A YEAR IN THE LIFE OF THE

CUNARD
FLEET

A YEAR IN THE LIFE OF THE
CUNARD FLEET

Sharon Poole and Andrew Sassoli-Walker

AMBERLEY

First published 2015

Amberley Publishing
The Hill, Stroud
Gloucestershire, GL5 4EP

www.amberley-books.com

British Library Cataloguing in Publication Data.
A catalogue record for this book is available from the British Library.

ISBN 978 1 4456 4609 1 (print)
ISBN 978 1 4456 4610 7 (ebook)

Typeset in 10pt on 12pt Celeste OT.
Typesetting and Origination by Amberley Publishing.
Printed in the UK.

CONTENTS

FOREWORD

At the tender age of seventeen, Samuel Cunard was already showing a keen business acumen in running his own general store in Halifax, Nova Scotia, Canada. Shortly afterwards he joined his father's timber business, and then expanded into coal, iron and shipping, investing in the steamship *Royal William*. In 1840 he co-founded the British & North American Royal Mail Steam Packet Co. and *Britannia* sailed from Liverpool to Halifax with the man himself on board, and sixty-three other passengers, and so began one of the most famous shipping companies in history.

The company made ocean liners a success in the face of many potential rivals, and his direction to his captains at the time was to always make safe passage and let others worry about speed and luxury, a safety legacy which indeed is upheld to this day. The ships of the Cunard Line became household names, *Mauretania*, *Queen Mary*, *Caronia* and *QE2*, to name but a few icons of the sea, a heritage that stands today with *Queen Mary 2*, *Queen Victoria* and *Queen Elizabeth*.

This is a company that has survived through wars, financial crises, the arrival of jet travel, and yet had the ability to change to reflect the needs of the sea-going traveller. They make going to sea in a Cunarder a great experience; as the advertisers said, 'Getting there is half the fun!'

I am extremely proud to have played a small part in the company history, and I hope this book will allow a glimpse of what we shared at sea in a Cunard liner.

Ian McNaught

Captain Ian McNaught MNM
Deputy Master
Trinity House

Captain Ian McNaught in the Captain's Dayroom on *QE2*. (Ian McNaught)

INTRODUCTION

It is no idle claim that Cunard's advertising boasts of having 'The Most Famous Ocean Liners in the World'. The company has given us some of the best-known and best-loved ships that ever sailed, their distinctive livery making them instantly recognisable all over the world. Ask anyone to name a passenger liner and most will come up with *Queen Elizabeth 2* or *Queen Mary*. Go back a little further and some of the most famous ships of their day were Cunarders – *Mauretania*, *Aquitania* and *Berengaria* to name a few.

In 1840 Cunard became the first company to offer passengers a regular scheduled transatlantic steamship service between the UK and North America. 175 years on, Cunard still provide what is now the only regular transatlantic crossing by sea, operating not only the youngest fleet afloat, but the last true ocean liner in the unique *Queen Mary 2*.

Over the years Cunard liners have played their part in history. *Carpathia* was the first ship to reach the survivors of the *Titanic*; *Lusitania* was torpedoed by a German U-boat in 1915, an event widely believed to have encouraged the USA to enter the First World War; Winston Churchill sailed on the *Queen Mary* when meeting the US President to agree details of Operation Overlord (D-Day) and the cream of Hollywood have been photographed on board as they travel to promote their latest film.

Nowadays, much of the fleet's time is spent cruising but Cunard's advertising slogan is still as relevant today as when it was first coined.

The iconic Cunard funnel livery, recognised all over the world. (Andrew Sassoli-Walker)

Queen Elizabeth leads *Queen Victoria* and *Queen Mary 2* out of Southampton on 13 July 2012. (Andrew Sassoli-Walker)

Chapter 1

A BRIEF HISTORY OF THE CUNARD LINE

Samuel Cunard was born in Halifax, Nova Scotia, on 21 November 1787. He, his father and brothers all built up successful businesses, so what made this fifty-two-year-old prosperous and conservative family man risk everything and move his family to Britain? The impetus was a small newspaper advertisement placed by the British Admiralty in 1839, inviting bids to operate a regular transatlantic steamship service to carry the Royal Mail between Britain and the North American continent.

Sailing ships took up to six weeks to reach Canada, then under British rule. However, following the successful use of steam in carrying the Royal Mail east to India, and two transatlantic crossings by the steamers *Sirius* and *Great Western* in 1838, the British Government invited tenders for transporting the North American mails. Despite having little experience with steam, then a rapidly developing technology, Cunard grasped the opportunity with both hands.

In search of capital, he sailed to Britain, then the foremost country in the world in the development of steam power. This led to a meeting with two ship owners, George Burns of Glasgow and David MacIver of Liverpool, both engaged in the coasting trade around the British Isles.

With the additional help of Clyde shipbuilder Robert Napier, the four men established the British & North American Royal Mail Steam Packet Co. Cunard returned to London and submitted his tender. It was a huge leap of faith, taking into account the financial penalties within the contract for late delivery and notwithstanding the fact that he did not possess any suitable steamships at that time. To back his offer, however, he had had discussions with Robert Napier over his requirements for four 1,120-ton steamers, subject to him winning the contract. Other potential bidders could not meet the Admiralty's tight timescales and Cunard's bid was accepted.

The Contract for the Conveyance of North American Mails, signed on 4 July 1839, specified that Cunard run a fortnightly service between Liverpool and Halifax, Nova Scotia. On arrival a smaller vessel was to 'proceed direct to Boston aforesaid, with the mails and despatches for that place on board, where such last-named vessel shall remain for the purpose of receiving any return mails'.

Another branch service carried mail to Montreal. Should weather or other issues prevent the eastbound ship making Liverpool, a further

This statue of Sir Samuel Cunard, by local sculptor Peter Bustin, was unveiled on the waterfront at Halifax, Nova Scotia, on 7 October 2006. One of the main instigators of this memorial was Commodore Ron Warwick, for many years master of both *QE2* and *QM2*. (Sharon Poole)

clause allowed the British naval officer on board to specify one of seven alternative ports – Bristol, Falmouth, Plymouth, Southampton, Portsmouth, Dover or Deal. All Royal Mail ships carried a naval officer solely responsible for the mail.

Launched in February 1840, *Britannia* was the first of the four vessels ordered. Built at R. Duncan & Co.'s yard at Greenock, Scotland, *The Times* reported on her launch and naming by Miss Isabella Napier. They described the vessel:

> Her length from taffrail to figurehead is 230 ft, the breadth of her beam is 31ft and the depth of her hold, 22ft 6in. She is to be propelled by two engines, each 22 horse-power, and when put to sea will be succeeded by three other ships of the same dimensions and similar construction ... The vessel's hull and machinery are constructed under the direction and superintendence of Mr Robert Napier of the Vulcan Foundry, Glasgow ... The accommodation of the vessel is provided on an improved and magnificent scale, the cabin below deck being fitted up with spacious and well-ventilated state-rooms. The dining-saloon is unique, and we may safely say that, from the keel to the topmast, everything will be found substantial and adapted to the course the vessel is to take.

Despite the glowing references to the accommodation, these ships were primarily built to carry cargo and mail. Cunard had expressly requested a 'plain and comfortable boat, but not the least unnecessary expense for show'. Writer Charles Dickens travelled with his wife to Boston on *Britannia* in 1842 and was not impressed, describing his stateroom as 'a profoundly preposterous box!' Each cabin was separated from the next by a partition with a candle on the top shared with the adjacent cabin. There was a narrow berth with a straw mattress and one small cupboard. The vessels were fitted with masts and a full set of sails, not only to provide backup in case of engine failure, but to supplement it when necessary and assist in stabilising the ship.

Britannia left Liverpool on 4 July 1840 and arrived in Halifax twelve days and ten hours later, an average speed of eight and a half knots. The three other ships, *Acadia, Caledonia* and *Columbia*, were launched soon after and a regular fortnightly schedule established.

1855 saw the launch of *Persia*, Cunard's first ocean-going steamship to be built entirely of iron. Iron ships were lighter and therefore could be larger with a greater capacity. She was still paddle-driven and it was only under intense competition that Cunard sought permission from the government (required under the terms of the contract) to fit his mail steamers with the more efficient screw propulsion, *China* being the first of their ships so driven.

The mail contract subsidies might have paid costs but the profit lay in carrying cargo and passengers, particularly emigrants. In the early days the vessels were single class and everyone paid the same passage money. In 1850, when competition strengthened, Cunard brought in chief-cabin and second-cabin categories. In the lowest class only a narrow bunk was provided, the emigrants providing their own bedding and food, and occupying the lower decks in dormitories with communal eating and cooking areas. Not until the later nineteenth century were third-class four- and six-berth cabins introduced.

Samuel Cunard died in 1865. Twelve years later, the British & North American Royal Mail Steam Packet Company was registered under the Limited Liability Act, changing their name to the more manageable Cunard Steamship Company and introducing the logo of a lion rampant holding a globe, a version of which is still in use today. A prospectus was issued stating that 'the growing wants of the Company's transatlantic trade demands the acquisition of additional steamships of greater size and power, involving a cost for construction which might

Top: A print of *Britannia* leaving Liverpool on Cunard's first mail crossing on 4 July 1840. She arrived in Halifax, Nova Scotia, twelve days and ten hours later, averaging a speed of eight and a half knots. (Sharon Poole Collection)

Bottom: A contemporary print of the Cunard steamship *Persia,* launched in 1855. *Persia* was their first vessel built entirely of iron. (Sharon Poole Collection)

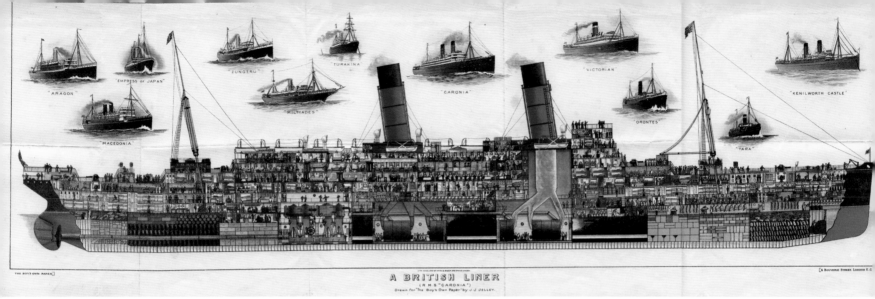

Section of the *Caronia*, drawn for *The Boy's Own Paper* in 1905 to illustrate the workings of a typical North Atlantic liner. Around one third of the interior space is taken up by the engines and cargo holds. Take away crew quarters and stores and it is easy to see why profit margins on passengers were so tight. (Sharon Poole Collection)

best be met by a large public company'. Additional routes were also added, such as a connecting service from New York to the West Indies via Nassau and Havana.

To attract passengers, ships became ever more elaborate and luxurious. In 1876 *Bothnia* was the first Cunarder to have a library and the introduction in 1881 of electric lighting on *Servia* marked a tremendous step forward, both in passenger comfort and safety. The crossing from Liverpool to New York now took less than six days in the fastest ships.

The 14,000-ton, twin-screw liners *Campania* and *Lucania*, launched in 1893, were milestones both in terms of size and speed. They were followed in 1904 by the 20,000-ton sisters *Caronia* and *Carmania*, the latter being the first of the company's ships to be powered by steam turbines. Passengers were now able to read news mid-Atlantic. The *Liverpool Courier* of 11 October 1904 reported:

The *Umbria* which sails from Liverpool for New York on the 15th instant, is at present being fitted with the Marconi long-distance wireless telegraphy apparatus, which will enable her to pick up etheric messages when 1,500 or 1,600 miles from land. During her forthcoming voyage, therefore, passengers by this steamer will be kept posted as to the world's happenings during the whole of the Atlantic trip. The news messages ... will be incorporated in the 'Cunard Daily Bulletin', a newspaper published on shipboard ...

The twentieth century saw the launches of the so-called ships of state, part-funded by governments to provide labour for shipyards, bring

Caronia, launched in July 1904. After service as a transatlantic liner, and an armed merchant cruiser during the First World War, she was converted for cruising in 1926, refitting the passenger accommodation to 452 cabin class, 365 tourist class and 650 third-class passengers. In January 1932 she was sold for scrap and broken up in Osaka, Japan. (Sharon Poole Collection)

Above: Lusitania, launched in 1907, is today mostly remembered for her sinking by a German submarine with the loss of 1,198 lives. Many of the dead were US citizens and this act is credited with bringing the USA into the First World War. (Sharon Poole Collection)

Below left: The first class dining saloon on *Aquitania*. (Sharon Poole collection)

prestige to the country and ensure a fleet of fast passenger vessels that could be requisitioned in times of war. The British government subsidised Cunard to the sum of £150,000 per annum to build two new express liners. The ships, to be named *Mauretania* and *Lusitania*, were fitted with steam-turbine engines, a comparatively new technology proven in *Carmania*, but fuelled by coal. However, they were designed for easy conversion to oil when a more reliable source became available at lower cost. *Lusitania* set sail on her maiden voyage on 7 September 1907, with *Mauretania* following on 16 November that year. At almost 32,000 grt, *Mauretania* was then the world's largest ship, with a top service speed of 25 knots. It was her speed and tight turning circle that were to save her in later years, outmanoeuvring torpedoes in the First World War.

This pair of ocean greyhounds came to epitomise sea travel at its grandest. In first class, everyone dressed for dinner and dined in elaborate saloons. They were warmed by real fires in open fireplaces and danced to live bands, cocooned in their own floating world for five days. Those travelling first class were the icing on the cake of profit, though, as the money still lay in emigrants, where quantity (of passengers) outranked quality of accommodation.

In 1911, *Franconia* became the first Cunarder built for both crossings and cruising and boasted the first on-board gymnasium as well as hot and cold running water in every cabin. The same year, Cunard purchased three new vessels to service a new route between London, Southampton and Canada. This heralded the beginning of the company's long association with Southampton.

We cannot travel past 1912 without mention of probably the most famous maritime disaster – the sinking of *Titanic*. White Star Line already held the record for owning the largest ship to founder at sea, when *Republic* was rammed by the Italian vessel *Florida* in thick fog in 1909. However, they would break their own record three years later when

Titanic hit that fateful iceberg. The closest ship at the time was Cunard's *Carpathia*, whose wireless operator picked up the distress signal at 00:15. He immediately woke the master, Captain Rostron, who promptly changed course and ordered all possible speed. At 04:00 *Carpathia* arrived at *Titanic*'s last known position to find just floating wreckage, bodies and 705 cold, wet and frightened survivors. With every survivor on board, the ship returned to New York from whence she came. Six weeks later Rostron and his crew were presented with special medals by those he rescued. Today, the White Star flag is raised on all Cunard ships every 15 April in memory of *Titanic*.

In 1913 another record-breaking ship was launched. *Aquitania* was built, without government subsidy, at John Brown's yard in Clydebank. At 45,647 grt, she was larger but otherwise similar in appearance to *Lusitania*, with four huge, raked funnels. Built at a cost of over £2 million, she boasted a Turkish bath, indoor swimming pool, cafes, theatre and gymnasium.

Like many merchant shipping lines, Cunard contributed vessels to campaigns from the Crimean War onwards; it was for service in that conflict that Samuel was knighted in 1859.

Some of the company's greatest losses fell during the First World War, when 56 per cent of their tonnage was sunk. One of the first vessels to be requisitioned was *Aquitania*. In just four days in the Mersey she was converted into a patrol vessel with eight six-inch guns mounted on her decks. The following year she transferred to trooping, carrying some 30,000 soldiers to the Dardanelles, after which she became a hospital ship until 1918, when she carried over 60,000 US troops to Europe. *Aquitania* survived not only the First World War, but also the Second World War, becoming one of Cunard's longest serving vessels.

In 1915 *Lucania* was converted into a seaplane carrier and made history as the first ship to launch an aircraft while underway. The same

Franconia, built in 1911, was the first Cunard liner built for both line voyages and summer cruising and had the first on-board gymnasium, pictured here. (Sharon Poole Collection)

year saw *Lusitania* sunk by a German submarine off the Old Head of Kinsale in Ireland.

A contemporary account by a passenger brings that day to life:

There was a fairly heavy fog early on Friday morning [7 May]. I was awakened about 7 o'clock by the blowing of the siren ... About noon the ship turned northward from the course she had been holding, making a huge semicircle and heeling well over to port. We had no notion why this was done, but at the time we wondered if news of a submarine had been received. I was on deck on the starboard side aft ... when I saw what looked like a whale or a porpoise rising about three-quarters of a mile to starboard ... Immediately a white line, a train of bubbles, started away from the black object ... It was aimed ahead and struck under the bridge ... The explosion came clear up through the upper deck and pieces of the wreckage fell clean aft of where we were standing ... There was no second torpedo, but the boilers exploded immediately. The passengers all rushed at once to the high side of the deck – the port side ... The first boat dropped clear of the ship with no-one in it ... Several other boats followed, and most of the people on that side got in them ... The second-class passengers swarmed over on to the first-cabin deck, and they helped to make the lack of life-preservers. *Lusitania* listed to starboard, and settled down on that side, also by the head, and as I went over the side and was dragged into a small boat it looked as if its smokestack [funnel] was going to hit us. But then the ship straightened up and rolled back to port and sank rapidly, bow first.

Of the 1,959 persons on board, 1,198 were lost, of which 128 were American citizens, their deaths encouraging the USA to enter the war. Controversy still reigns as to whether *Lusitania* was a legitimate target, although she was carrying munitions amongst her cargo at the time.

Carpathia, heroine of the *Titanic* disaster, was sunk by three torpedoes just two months before the war ended. *Ausonia* was particularly unlucky in that she was torpedoed – twice! The first time a torpedo took off her rudder and both propellers, but she stayed afloat long enough for emergency repairs to get her under tow to Bristol, where a new stern was fitted. Almost exactly a year later, she was hit again. All but eight of the crew managed to take to the boats before the submarine surfaced and sank *Ausonia* with shell fire.

These are the war stories of just a few of Cunard's ships and crew but many more were equally courageous under fire. Sixteen of their ships were lost due to wartime action.

As well as 'active service', Cunarders transported over nine and a half million tons of foodstuffs, munitions and general goods. The company also assisted the war effort by building England's largest aircraft factory of the time at Aintree, turning their engineering works on Merseyside into a munitions factory and by using their huge laundry to service Red Cross hospitals.

When peace returned Cunard, like all other lines, had to rebuild its fleet. As well as refitting ships as they were released by the government, they were awarded the German liner *Imperator* in reparation for *Lusitania*, renaming her *Berengaria*.

In 1919 the home port for the express service was moved from Liverpool to Southampton, although the company's headquarters remained on the Pier Head at Liverpool until 1967. No longer used by Cunard, the waterfront buildings and old docks are now a UNESCO World Heritage site.

Mauretania suffered a fire in 1921, so Cunard took the opportunity to give the ship a complete overhaul and upgrade, including converting her engines to burn oil. The changes made her ideal to start a programme of winter cruises to the Mediterranean, together with *Aquitania*. A major factor in this decision was the US Immigration Restriction Act of 1921, which limited the numbers of immigrants the country would accept. The classes were re-organised for cruising and tourist third-class was born.

In 1930, the traditional Cunard livery of a dark grey/black hull was changed to all white for cruising. During these years of Prohibition in the USA, the fact that the ships sold alcohol proved a valuable selling point and *Berengaria* was used for short party cruises along the US coast. In his memoir, *The Sea My Surgery*, Dr Joseph Maguire writes of Winston Churchill tendering ashore at Nassau 'surrounded by drunken American gangsters and bootleggers and their giggling women'. Alcohol was sold as soon as the ship was outside the three-mile limit and bar takings alone for these three-day cruises could be around £7,500.

By 1933 the Depression was taking its toll. Work had been paused in 1931 on Cunard's new liner, *Queen Mary*. The British government agreed

Left: Berengaria was launched as *Imperator* in 1912, for the Hamburg America Line. She was awarded to Cunard after the First World War as reparation for the loss of *Lusitania*. (Sharon Poole Collection)

Below left: Begun in 1914, Cunard Line's headquarters remained on the Pier Head at Liverpool until 1967. Today this building, together with the Royal Liver Building and the Port of Liverpool Building either side – the Three Graces – are together a Liverpool World Heritage site. (Sharon Poole)

Below: QM2 is fêted on her maiden visit to Liverpool, one of the ports on her first Round Britain cruise, October 2009. (Cunard)

Plan of the tourist third-class accommodation on *Berengaria* in March 1929. (Sharon Poole collection)

to provide assistance to both Cunard and their competitor, White Star Line, on condition they merge their North Atlantic operations, creating Cunard White Star Line Ltd on 10 May 1934. *Mauretania*'s last voyage was in September 1934 – the same month that *Queen Mary* was launched on Clydebank. Prior to being sold for scrap, an auction was held on board in Southampton, with whole rooms of panelling, fixtures and fittings going under the hammer. Some of these can still be seen today, for example in the Mauretania Bar and Lounge in Bristol.

Aquitania had a longer service life. The only Cunarder to serve in both World Wars, she was scrapped in 1950. The third ship in this pre-war group, *Berengaria*, was decommissioned in 1938 and, like *Mauretania*, her interiors were auctioned off.

Following the merger of Cunard and White Star, and with an upturn in the economy, work resumed on *Queen Mary*, with a launch by HM the Queen on 26 September 1934. This was the first of Cunard's ships to be named by a member of the royal family – a tradition maintained ever since. Plans were also made for another new liner – *Queen Elizabeth* – to be launched in 1940, Cunard's centenary year.

Queen Mary was 81,327 grt. To provide an optical illusion of streamlining, her three funnels, each 30 feet in diameter, decreased in height from fore to aft. She had twelve public decks, with accommodation for cabin, tourist and third-class passengers. Amenities included a swimming pool, Turkish and curative baths, shopping centre, bank and garage. It was calculated that two ships of her size could maintain a service previously operated by three vessels, so streamlining operations and cutting costs. Transatlantic one-way fares in the summer ranged from $316 for first-class to $107.50 for third-class.

To accommodate the two new ships, more extensive port facilities were required at Southampton. The King George V Graving Dock was built and the Upper Swinging Ground widened to enable these huge liners

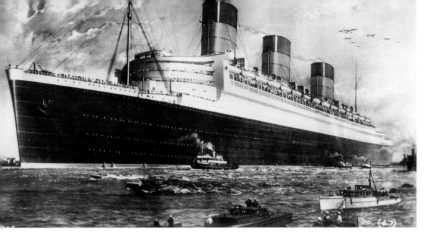

Above: Queen Mary, then the world's largest and fastest liner, was launched on the Clyde on 26 September 1934 by HM the Queen. (Sharon Poole Collection)

Right: Third-class stateroom on *Queen Mary*. (Sharon Poole Collection)

Far right above: Cabin-class stateroom on *Queen Mary*. Note the twin portholes. (Sharon Poole Collection)

Far right below: Tourist-class dining saloon on *Queen Mary* in the late 1940s. (Sharon Poole Collection)

Above left: A Southern Railway Class S15 4-6-0 steam locomotive with *QE2*. The SR was originally the owner of Southampton Docks, and ran regular express services from London Waterloo direct to the Cunard liners at the original Ocean Terminal. (Andrew Sassoli-Walker)

Above right: At the height of the summer season, *Queen Victoria* manoeuvres in the Upper Swinging Ground in Southampton, before berthing at the Mayflower Cruise Terminal, while *QM2* turns in the Lower Swinging Ground for the Ocean Terminal. (Andrew Sassoli-Walker)

to turn before berthing – a facility still in use today. From this date, the Hampshire port overtook Liverpool as the main base for the company.

As *Queen Mary* was under construction some masters commented that they had enough worry in a ship of 35,000 tons let alone her 81,237 grt. However, following sea trials, her first master, Commodore Sir Edgar Britten, stated he had never known a ship 'so amenable, so responsive, so sweet-tempered'. This was particularly appreciated by Captain Donald Sorrell, who, during the New York waterfront strike of 1945, achieved what the Manhattan longshoremen thought impossible, and berthed *Queen Mary* without the assistance of tugs or stevedores and without a scratch!

At the outbreak of the Second World War *Queen Elizabeth* was still lying unfinished at John Brown's yard at Clydebank, presenting not just an enemy target, but taking up space urgently needed for warships. *Queen Mary*, meanwhile, had been laid up at New York. It was decided that *Queen Elizabeth* should join her. She was taken by tugs downriver to the anchorage at Gourock then, under cover of darkness, slipped anchor and sailed under her own – untested – steam ostensibly to Southampton but in fact made the run across the Atlantic, arriving in New York on 7 March 1940. So secret had been her crossing, and so silent her arrival, that even Cunard White Star staff at their offices at 25 Broadway were as astounded as locals to wake up to see this huge liner berthed at Manhattan. *Queen Mary* then sailed to Australia, where she was converted into a troopship, leaving two weeks later with 5,000 ANZAC troops to bring back to Britain. As the theatre of war spread, she then sailed, in convoy with, among others, *Aquitania* and the new *Mauretania*, to the Middle East.

In the meantime *Queen Elizabeth* was repainted in camouflage and pressed into service as a trooper. By the end of 1941 the two Queens had ferried over 80,000 soldiers between Australia and North Africa. Return trips brought wounded and prisoners of war, and so the shuttle service continued – until the Japanese bombed the US naval base at Pearl Harbor and brought the Americans into the war.

Queen Elizabeth made all possible speed across the Pacific to Vancouver, refuelling en route at the remote Marquesas Islands, where a tanker had been sent to meet her, then to San Francisco, where her interior was virtually gutted, and finally to New York. *Queen Mary* had already been fitted with extra bunks in every possible corner – even the emptied indoor swimming pools! What followed was an astounding operation to shuttle US troops, up to 15,000 at a time, secretly to the UK until the end of the war. The vessels had only speed to keep them safe from submarines; the same speed denied them the comfort of escorting warships, who could not keep up the thirty knots they maintained every crossing.

Dr Joseph Maguire describes the process of embarkation in his book, *The Sea My Surgery*. Across the Hudson River in New Jersey men received final training.

There, completely hidden from the public eye, enormous wooden mock-ups of the sides of the two ships had been specially built on land. Time after time the men ... marched up to whichever numbered gangway they had been allotted to on the real ship. They then 'went below' to mocked-up decks, each section going straight to their allotted quarters represented by squares marked off behind framework. ... The result was that when sailing time came the men knew exactly where to go and what to do. No troops for overseas set foot in New York City. They entrained for Hoboken Terminal which was barred to the public. There they filed straight from the trains to the ferries where they went below decks, out of sight. The ferries carried them alongside the end of Pier 90 where one or other of the Queens lay ... Each section marched straight to its numbered gangway and boarded the ship. More, they moved, when inboard, straight to the part of the vessel allotted to them, which they had never seen but which was as well-known to them as their own home back yard ... No troops were allowed on deck until we had passed Sandy Hook and the pilot had been dropped.

Every crossing followed a different course and every time more and more soldiers were packed on board, until eventually the men had to operate a rota system to sleep. Water was strictly rationed and the GIs could only be fed twice a day in six sittings per meal.

Nearly two million troops were carried east across the Atlantic by the two Queens alone, in complete secrecy and safety. On one voyage in July 1943, *Queen Mary* carried the greatest number of people ever on board a ship – 15,740 troops and 943 crew.

Many other Cunard ships played a vital wartime role, some of them paying the ultimate price – the *Laurentic*, *Andania*, *Laconia* (1921), *Carinthia* and *Lancastria* (1924), but the contribution by the two most famous of the fleet was incalculable. It is no exaggeration when it is said that the two Queens shortened the duration of the war by a year.

After the war, troops and prisoners of war needed repatriation and American and Canadian war brides and their children were carried to their new homes in North America so it was a while before the liners re-entered civilian service. *Queen Elizabeth* was finally completed and painted in the traditional Cunard livery for the first time. One poignant reminder of her

Above left: RMS *Lancastria* was requisitioned as a troopship during the Second World War. She was sunk while evacuating troops and civilian refugees from France in 1940. It was the greatest ever loss of life in the sinking of a single British ship, more than the combined losses of *Titanic* and *Lusitania*. This plaque is on the waterfront at Liverpool opposite the Cunard Building. (Sharon Poole)

Above: A Cunard advertising poster, showing the whole post-war passenger fleet. (Sharon Poole Collection)

Left: The tourist-class Winter Gardens on *Queen Elizabeth* in the 1950s. They bear a striking resemblance to the Winter Garden on *QM2* today. (Sharon Poole Collection)

wartime years was preserved – a portion of the teak Boat Deck handrail, in which some of the soldiers had carved their names or initials.

By the late 1950s many travellers began to fly rather than sail across the ocean, although Cunard still had twelve ships deployed on transatlantic routes. This decade was one of the toughest for the company. Fares had doubled in the post-war years and there were strict curbs on the amount of cash that could be taken out of the UK. The McCarran Act was passed in the USA, to prevent entry to communists, anarchists and other undesirables. This meant long hours of screening for both passengers and crew before disembarkation in New York. Cunard started to market a transatlantic crossing as a holiday in its own right rather than just a means of travel. They also began to offer more cruises, as well as entering the containerisation revolution by becoming a member of the Atlantic Container Lines consortium for cargo services in 1966. However, the biggest problem with using liners as cruise ships is that cruising is a classless holiday, whereas the ships were designed for two- or three-class crossings.

Above left: A postcard of *Queen Mary* from 1967. Despite clearly being of another age, she was still plying the North Atlantic route, even as air travel was taking her custom. (Sharon Poole Collection)

Above right: *QM2* meets her older namesake *Queen Mary* for the first time at Long Beach, California, on 23 February 2006. (Bernard Warner)

In the mid-1960s, *Queen Mary* and *Queen Elizabeth* were still plying the North Atlantic even as air travel finally overtook sea travel in popularity. Cunard withdrew from a year-round service in 1968 to concentrate on cruising and summer transatlantic crossings for tourists. *Queen Mary* was retired in 1967 and *Queen Elizabeth* in 1968. While the former is preserved as a hotel and visitor attraction in Long Beach, California, the latter ended up in Hong Kong to be converted into *Seawise University*. However, fire broke out during the conversion and the vessel was destroyed.

Once or twice in a generation a ship comes along that becomes a legend in her own lifetime. For Cunard it was *Queen Elizabeth 2* (*QE2*).

The original plan had been to build two new liners to directly replace *Queen Mary* and *Queen Elizabeth*. However, a government committee headed by Lord Chandos felt this was uneconomically viable and agreed to fund just one new vessel of 75,000 tons. However, competition from aircraft and increases in operating costs for liners led to further doubts as to the practicality of the plan. Eventually a smaller liner was approved, with the ability to transit the Panama and Suez canals and which was suitable for extended periods of cruising. The government agreed to provide a loan on this basis. Hull No. Q4 was built at John Brown's shipyard on the Clyde, the same yard that produced *Lusitania*, *Aquitania* and the two great Queens. Launched on 20 September 1967 by HM the Queen, QE2 became the longest-serving Cunard vessel to date and defied city analysts who predicted she would be mothballed within six months.

QE2 was built in the traditional method of steel plates welded to a steel frame, but that was where tradition ended. As the *Daily Telegraph* reported in 1968, 'There is nothing of the old lady about the new *Queen Elizabeth Two* [sic]. She is smart, crisp and modern'.

Flouting conventional transatlantic liner design, there was no indoor promenade deck at public room level, allowing Cunard to utilise the full width of the ship for lounges. In June 1971 a visitor called Jean sent a postcard to a friend and was clearly awed by the variety of entertainment and sports on offer, 'Here I am on the liner *Queen Elizabeth II* [sic] for the day. It's a wonderful boat and has just about everything on it. Drink, dance, plays, pool, playroom, gym, bowls, ping pong, boxing, darts, skittles, the lot.'

QE2 took to her multiple roles with grace and ease, becoming possibly the best-loved Cunarder ever. She was designed as a three-class ship, but

Above: QE2 at anchor at Bar Harbour, Maine, USA, September 2006. This shows her beautiful lines to perfection. (Sharon Poole)

Opposite page: Although somewhat cramped by today's standards, the bridge of *QE2* was state-of-the-art for her time. (Andrew Sassoli-Walker)

a late decision was made to reduce that to two classes. Since the designs were already in place, with the main lounge of each class directly above each other, it was fairly simple to remove most of the floor area of the uppermost lounge and build a staircase linking it with the room below – so forming the famous Double Room. Unusually, the cabin-class lounge was the lowest of the three – the famous Queens Room directly below the Double Room.

In 1971 Cunard was bought by the conglomerate Trafalgar House. One major difference between a passenger liner and a cruise ship is that a cruise ship carries no cargo or mail so all profit has to come from heads and must counter operating costs – wages, berthing fees, food, maintenance and, most expensive of all, fuel. In 1973 and 1974, fuel oil costs rose four-fold, putting cruising from the UK into serious doubt, especially using converted liners who tended to be heavy on fuel

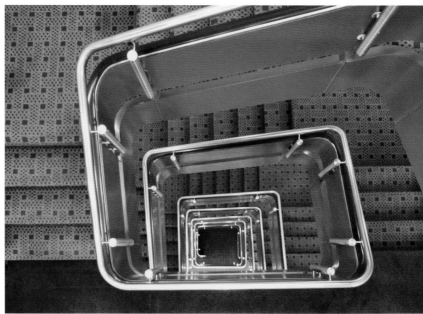

Above left: The stern of the Promenade Deck of *QE2* at night in October 2008. (Sharon Poole)

Above right: Stairway A on *QE2* connected the lowest passenger deck up to Boat Deck. A relic from her days as a two-class liner, it gave limited access to decks in between. (Sharon Poole)

and carry fewer passengers than cruise ships. Trafalgar House wasted no time in consolidating the company's position in the market, disposing of most of the cargo fleet and bringing in Cunard's first dedicated cruise ships – *Cunard Adventurer* and *Cunard Ambassador*. Realising they had delayed entry into this market too long, they bought into existing orders, forming a partnership with Overseas National Airways, who later withdrew, leaving the ships under sole Cunard ownership. At just over 14,000 grt, they were designed with economy in mind and carried around 800 passengers, mostly on seven-day fly-cruises around the Caribbean. Both ships suffered mechanical issues and when *Ambassador* had an engine-room fire in 1974, she was sold. *Adventurer* was sold in 1976, when they were replaced with two new, slightly larger, cruise ships – *Cunard Countess* and *Cunard Princess*, both 17,586 grt. These vessels operated seven-night Caribbean cruises, alternating two itineraries so passengers could book a back-to-back fourteen-night cruise. In the summer, one ship repositioned to Alaska.

Texan Linda Lee recalls of *Cunard Countess*:

I remember sitting on Pool Deck facing the smokestack [funnel] which was painted white. The tropical sun was so intense that my eyes kept closing from the glare. I finally had to go below-decks and get my sunglasses. My memory of the lobby and reception desk (a double Dutch-door with one person stationed inside) was of the colour royal blue – drapes, carpeting, sofa, walls, all were royal blue. It was like walking into a cave. The hotel crew were younger and quite fun for the teenage grandkids. The cruise director hung out behind the double Dutch-door and dispensed shore excursion advice while trying to upsell those visits.

Cunard Countess Caribbean Cruises

New Holidays via Barbados in 1985
Cunard Countess continues her popular itineraries round the pick of the Caribbean islands in 1985 but with an exciting new holiday option – a two week holiday with direct return flights to join the ship in Barbados.

Flights are on the scheduled British Airways service from London Heathrow and connect the same day with Cunard Countess. The cruise itinerary starting in Barbados visits Martinique, St. Thomas, San Juan, Tortola, Nevis, St. Kitts, Guadeloupe, St. Lucia, St. Maarten, La Guaira (for Caracas), Grenada and finally returns to Barbados a fortnight later for the homeward flight.

Departures for these holidays are fortnightly on Wednesdays starting on January 9 and prices are from £1,125 per person.

Honeymooners!
A Caribbean cruise is a thrilling idea for a honeymoon or can make a wedding anniversary a very special occasion.

So if you're just married or your anniversary falls during your cruise, we'll provide a

complimentary bottle of wine and a special cake to help you celebrate.

Full details are in the new Cunard Countess brochure – fill in the coupon on the back of this newsletter for your copy.

The brochure also contains details of Cunard Countess cruises from San Juan already established for a number of years, and cruise and stay holidays combining one week aboard Cunard Countess and one week ashore either at Paradise Beach Hotel on Barbados or La Toc on St. Lucia.

Cunard Princess The Best of West Coast America

Summer Cruises to Alaska
Cunard Princess, now based permanently on the west coast of America, offers in the summer months May to September the best Alaska cruise itinerary available. Departing from Vancouver on Saturday, she travels far enough north in 7 days to view the most spectacular glaciers in North America - the Columbia and Hubbard Glaciers, as well as seven others – and have a day in Anchorage Alaska's largest metropolis.

She then sails south again giving passengers a second chance to see one of the most scenic coastlines in the world. Ports of call include Ketchikan with its impressive totem pole collection; Juneau Alaska's scenic capital and Skagway the pioneer gold rush town and gateway to the Klondike.

Flights to and from Vancouver and an overnight stay in this city are all included in the price for this thrilling and unusual holiday.

Mexican Winter Sunshine
Three days in Acapulco with Cunard Princess as your luxury hotel is the highspot of the ship's regular two week Mexican cruise programme which operates from September to April. This jet set resort offers white sand beaches, shopping for handicrafts, sightseeing like a trip to the cliffs of "La Quebrada" to see divers plunging to the sea and dazzling evening entertainment including flamenco shows, nightclubs and discos.

Other ports of call are Mazatlan where a Rodeo and Fiesta of Mexican songs and dances is organised for cruise passengers, Manzanillo where seafood restaurants offer tasty local dishes and Puerto Vallarta with palm fringed beaches and an attractive waterfront boulevard. All are set in lush tropical scenery in the sunny, colourful atmosphere of the Mexican Riviera - a perfect escape from the cold of a British winter.

With prices in 1985 starting at £1,175 per person – a reduction on 1984 rates – including return flights to Los Angeles to join the ship these holidays are an excellent bargain. Full details are in the Cunard Countess Caribbean brochure.

A page advertising Caribbean cruises on *Cunard Countess*, from the *Cunard World* magazine for past passengers, November 1984. (Sharon Poole Collection)

In the spring of 1982 Cunard once again were called upon to assist the UK in time of conflict. Argentina's new head of their military junta, General Galtieri, tried to divert attention away from domestic problems and unite the country behind his plan to regain what Argentina called Las Islas Malvinas and which Britain knew as the Falkland Islands. He believed Britain would surrender the islands, especially in view of the logistical problems fighting a war so distant and in an Antarctic winter. The British Prime Minister at the time, the late Margaret Thatcher, wasn't giving in so easily and, while attempts were made for a peaceful resolution, a plan was put together to recapture the islands.

To move people and equipment such a distance, civilian ships would be required, of which a number came from Cunard. Two in particular would be remembered. The container ship *Atlantic Conveyor* of Cunard subsidiary Atlantic Container Line was converted to transport Harrier vertical-take-off aircraft and helicopters, together with armaments, vehicles, stores and other equipment. On 25 May she was hit by two Argentinian Exocet missiles. After valiant efforts from her civilian crew, the vessel was abandoned, with the loss of twelve lives. Despite attempts to salvage her, she eventually succumbed to the sea.

The most notable Cunard vessel requisitioned was *QE2*. News of the requisitioning came as a surprise to the crew, who heard about it on the BBC news the day the ship arrived back in Southampton from Philadelphia, where she had been for the city's tercentennial celebrations. Immediately her lines were made fast, *QE2* was officially handed over. It was 4 May 1982.

The speed of the conversion was staggering, plans having been drawn up in advance while the ship was still mid-Atlantic. Open deck areas were converted to become helipads and provision was made for refuelling at sea, a necessity given the distance to the South Atlantic. Over 1,000 of her crew volunteered to sail on this extraordinary voyage, of which approximately 650 were chosen, under the command of Captain Peter Jackson. Eight days later, *QE2* set sail with 3,000 troops on board, watched by hundreds of well-wishers ashore and afloat. What few realised was that two of the three boilers were still under maintenance, but due to publicity pressure to show the ship departing on schedule, this was completed with the ship at anchor out of sight, south of the Isle of Wight, before continuing her voyage the following morning.

One major challenge was to enforce total blackout conditions, a task and a half for a passenger liner! In addition they had to operate without radar to avoid detection by the enemy. As *QE2* sailed further south, the severity of the conflict increased, with losses of a number of ships, including *Atlantic Conveyor*. The tension was compounded by increasing ice which, combined with bad visibility, meant the radar had to be switched back on. Captain Jackson described having to negotiate icebergs, including one over a mile long and 300 feet high, as the most harrowing experience he had ever encountered in forty years at sea.

Such a famous ship would have made a valuable prize, so it was decided that *QE2* would not travel to the islands themselves, but would transfer the troops to other vessels at South Georgia. She arrived on 27 May at Cumberland Bay, to a somewhat surreal meeting with P&O's requisitioned liner *Canberra*. All the troops were transferred to *Canberra*, exchanging them for survivors of HMS *Ardent*, HMS *Coventry* and HMS *Antelope*. *QE2* then put to sea, once again negotiating the ice fields. Initial plans were to disembark the survivors at Ascension Island before sailing south again, but the Ministry of Defence decided that *QE2* would sail straight home to Southampton. Her arrival back in the Solent was, like all the homecomings from the conflict, an amazing spectacle, with people lining the banks at every vantage point, as a flotilla of small boats escorted the vessel back into Southampton.

The aft heli-pad

During the night of 26 and 27 May the radar was switched on every 30 minutes and at one time more than 100 icebergs could be seen on the screen. Captain Jackson would later write that "never have I known such a harrowing experience".

ain Jackson later commented: "We knew we were a e target and I'm thankful they never found us... in the sea we were very vulnerable. We did not know where

QE2 to transfer yet more troops for the last time until morning when the operation would start again. From 0600 hours on 28 May the transfer from QE2 would start in earnest with helicopters, QE2's own lifeboats and the trawlers Cordella, Junella, Northella, Farnella and Pict carrying troops and stores to waiting Canberra and Norland, the latter bringing to QE2 survivors from HMS Antelope. Canberra sailed at 2230 hours as snow fell, covering the assembled ships.

The next day saw another Cunard cargo ship, Saxonia, and the Royal Fleet auxiliary Stromness rendezvous with QE2 and the auxiliary vessel brought survivors from HMS Coventry. Captain Jackson was concerned about the deteriorating weather and icebergs had drifted in and out of the entrance to Cumberland Bay during QE2's stay there. Junella took the

QE2 and as the ship passed the Needles Lighthouse at 0900 hours the Royal Yacht Britannia came abeam with The Queen Mother standing on the aft deck. QE2's crew and warship survivors gave three cheers and the liner blew her whistle in salute.

As QE2 made her way to her berth she was escorted by a flotilla of small craft and thousands cheered and waved from the shore as she berthed. QE2 had sailed the 6,796 mile distance from South Georgia to Southampton in 12 days, 12 hours and 18 minutes at an average speed of 23.23 knots.

On 13 June Admiral Sir Henry Leach wrote to Captain Jackson: "...I wanted to let you know how very grateful I and the whole Navy have been for your splendid and efficient help over the recent weeks. As you will know better

QE2 in Cumberland Bay

The Falklands Remembered

DINNER ON BOARD
QUEEN ELIZABETH 2
WEDNESDAY 19 SEPTEMBER 2007

MOST FAMOUS OCEAN LINERS IN THE WORLD™

The Prime Minister Margaret Thatcher, whose government requisitioned QE2 for the Falklands War

an a one-way ng at sea. Pipes ge area on Two

were removed houses ashore. entertaining), d items were

the Double Down Bar, Casino and the Nursery.

A NAAFI Shop was installed in the Shopping Arcade selling cans of beer. The Cinema was rigged up for mass briefings. The Q4 Room became the Officers' Bar while the Theatre Bar became an NCO Bar. The One Deck Shop became a Library. The various offices around the ship as well as the Reading Room, Card Room and Library became official meeting rooms.

On 12 May, eight days after arriving in Southampton, th formal embarkation of the 3,000 troops that made up Infantry Brigade began. The Brigade comprised the Scot Guards, the Welsh Guards and the Ghurka Rifles. Bands o pipers were on hand playing as each unit boarded and b early afternoon the Brigade was all on board. A large crow and a posse of television cameras had assembled on th quayside. QE2 was ready to go to war. But not before th Cunard Chairman Lord Matthews and the Defence Ministe

n 19 March 1982 the Argentine army invaded the British colony of the Falkland Islands in the uth Atlantic. Within days a task force ad been despatched and several ommercial vessels, including P&O's anberra, had been requisitioned and converted for war service.

Despite constant rumours that QE2 would also be 'called up' Cunard rebutted any such talk and the ship continued as scheduled with an Atlantic crossing to New York, followed by a maiden call to Philadelphia on 25 April where she officiated at the opening of the year-long tricentennial celebrations of the founding of the city in 1682.

A Sea-King helicopter collects more stores from the aft heli-pad

However, there was no doubting that QE2's speed, size and facilities made her ideal for trooping and on 3 May 1982, as QE2 was steaming along the south coast of England bound for Southampton, the long-expected news that she had been requisitioned by the British Government for use in the Falklands campaign was confirmed.

Cunard received the following instructions from the Government:

"Your vessel Queen Elizabeth 2 is requisitioned by the Secretary of State for Trade under the Requisitioning of Ships Order 1982 and you are accordingly required to place her at his disposal forthwith. The Master should report for directions on the employment of the vessel to

over the ship. All future sailings Cunard did not know for how requisitioned, but it was felt tha them within two months.

QE2 officially came alongside h May and was immediately req becoming a 'STUFT' (Ship Taken hours that evening, after passeng normal cleaning-up chores ha swung the liner-cum-troopship a so that her starboard side la conversion work began on 5 May trooping assignment and over th amazing transformation took pla

QE2's aft decks became helicop extensive alterations were unde away large parts of the superstru was extended towards the bow that a third heli-pad could be bu new landing pads were capable pounds of a Sea King helicopter have had to carry.

The heli-pads were pre-fabricated Vosper Thorneycroft yard and the for installation which involved a

The Falklands Conflict remembered in a special menu for passengers on *QE2*'s fortieth year in service cruise. (Mark Thomas collection)

Above left: After her 1982 voyage to the South Atlantic as part of Operation Corporate, *QE2* arrives in the King George V Graving Dock for a refit before returning to service. This dry dock was originally built in 1933 for *Queen Mary* and *Queen Elizabeth*, when Cunard moved their flagship express service from Liverpool to Southampton. (Bob Walker)

Left: This large wooden plaque was presented to *QE2* by First Sea Lord Sir John Fieldhouse to commemorate the ship's service in the Falklands Conflict of 1982. (Sharon Poole)

Above: *Vistafjord* was one of the two ships that gave Cunard a foothold in the German cruise market when she was bought from Norwegian America Cruises. She is pictured passing P&O's *Canberra*. (Andrew Sassoli-Walker)

Opposite page: When converted from steam to diesel-electric power in 1986, *QE2* had a new, larger funnel which gave a powerful look to her profile. (Andrew Sassoli-Walker)

During the night of 26 and 27 May the radar was switched on every 30 minutes and at one time more than 100 icebergs could be seen on the screen. Captain Jackson would later write that "never have I known such a harrowing experience".

The aft heli-pad

...tain Jackson later commented: "We knew we were a ...me target and I'm thankful they never found us... in the ...en sea we were very vulnerable. We did not know where...

QE2 to transfer yet more troops for the last time until morning when the operation would start again. From 0600 hours on 28 May the transfer from QE2 would start in earnest with helicopters, QE2's own lifeboats and the trawlers Cordella, Junella, Northella, Farnella and Pict carrying troops and stores to waiting Canberra and Norland, the latter bringing to QE2 survivors from HMS Antelope. Canberra sailed at 2230 hours as snow fell, covering the assembled ships.

The next day saw another Cunard cargo ship, Saxonia, and the Royal Fleet auxiliary Stromness rendezvous with QE2 and the auxiliary vessel brought survivors from HMS Coventry. Captain Jackson was concerned about the deteriorating weather and icebergs had drifted in and out of the entrance to Cumberland Bay during QE2's stay there. Junella took the...

QE2 and as the ship passed the Needles Lighthouse at 0900 hours the Royal Yacht Britannia came abeam with The Queen Mother standing on the aft deck. QE2's crew and warship survivors gave three cheers and the liner blew her whistle in salute.

As QE2 made her way to her berth she was escorted by a flotilla of small craft and thousands cheered and waved from the shore as she berthed. QE2 had sailed the 6,796 mile distance from South Georgia to Southampton in 12 days, 12 hours and 18 minutes at an average speed of 23.23 knots.

On 13 June Admiral Sir Henry Leach wrote to Captain Jackson: "...I wanted to let you know how very grateful I and the whole Navy have been for your splendid and efficient help over the recent weeks. As you will know better...

QE2 in Cumberland Bay

The Falklands Remembered

DINNER ON BOARD
QUEEN ELIZABETH 2
WEDNESDAY 19 SEPTEMBER 2007

MOST FAMOUS OCEAN LINERS IN THE WORLD™

...han a one-way ...ng at sea. Pipes ...ge area on Two

...were removed ...houses ashore ...entertaining), ...d items were

the Double Down Bar, Casino and the Nursery.

A NAAFI Shop was installed in the Shopping Arcade selling cans of beer. The Cinema was rigged up for mass briefings. The Q4 Room became the Officers' Bar while the Theatre Bar became an NCO Bar. The One Deck Shop became a Library. The various offices around the ship as well as the Reading Room, Card Room and Library became official meeting rooms.

On 12 May, eight days after arriving in Southampton, th... formal embarkation of the 3,000 troops that made up ... Infantry Brigade began. The Brigade comprised the Scot... Guards, the Welsh Guards and the Ghurka Rifles. Bands o... pipers were on hand playing as each unit boarded and b... early afternoon the Brigade was all on board. A large crow... and a posse of television cameras had assembled on th... quayside. QE2 was ready to go to war. But not before th... Cunard Chairman Lord Matthews and the Defence Ministe...

On 19 March 1982 the Argentine army invaded the British colony of the Falkland Islands in the ...uth Atlantic. Within days a task force ...d been despatched and several ...ommercial vessels, including P&O's ...anberra, had been requisitioned and converted for war service.

Despite constant rumours that QE2 would also be 'called up' Cunard rebutted any such talk and the ship continued as scheduled with an Atlantic crossing to New York, followed by a maiden call to Philadelphia on 25 April where officiated at the opening of the year-long tricentennial celebrations of the founding of the city in 1682.

The Prime Minister Margaret Thatcher, whose government requisitioned QE2 for the Falklands War

A Sea-King helicopter collects more stores from the aft heli-pad

However, there was no doubting that QE2's speed, size and facilities made her ideal for trooping and on 3 May 1982, as QE2 was steaming along the south coast of England bound for Southampton, the long-expected news that she had been requisitioned by the British Government for use in the Falklands campaign was confirmed.

Cunard received the following instructions from the Government:

"Your vessel Queen Elizabeth 2 is requisitioned by the Secretary of State for Trade under the Requisitioning of Ships Order 1982 and you are accordingly required to place her at his disposal forthwith. The Master should report for directions on the employment of the vessel to...

over the ship. All future sailings... Cunard did not know for how... requisitioned, but it was felt tha... them within two months.

QE2 officially came alongside he... May and was immediately req... becoming a 'STUFT' (Ship Taken... hours that evening, after passeng... normal cleaning-up chores ha... swung the liner-cum-troopship a... so that her starboard side lay... conversion work began on 5 May... trooping assignment and over th... amazing transformation took pla...

QE2's aft decks became helicop... extensive alterations were unde... away large parts of the superstru... was extended towards the bow ... that a third heli-pad could be bu... new landing pads were capable ... pounds of a Sea King helicopter ... have had to carry.

The heli-pads were pre-fabricated... Vosper Thorneycroft yard and the... for installation which involved a...

The Falklands Conflict remembered in a special menu for passengers on *QE2*'s fortieth year in service cruise. (Mark Thomas collection)

Above left: After her 1982 voyage to the South Atlantic as part of Operation Corporate, *QE2* arrives in the King George V Graving Dock for a refit before returning to service. This dry dock was originally built in 1933 for *Queen Mary* and *Queen Elizabeth*, when Cunard moved their flagship express service from Liverpool to Southampton. (Bob Walker)

Left: This large wooden plaque was presented to *QE2* by First Sea Lord Sir John Fieldhouse to commemorate the ship's service in the Falklands Conflict of 1982. (Sharon Poole)

Above: Vistafjord was one of the two ships that gave Cunard a foothold in the German cruise market when she was bought from Norwegian America Cruises. She is pictured passing P&O's *Canberra*. (Andrew Sassoli-Walker)

Opposite page: When converted from steam to diesel-electric power in 1986, *QE2* had a new, larger funnel which gave a powerful look to her profile. (Andrew Sassoli-Walker)

After the end of the conflict, *Cunard Countess* was chartered for six months to ferry troops between Ascension Island and the Falkland Islands while Port Stanley Airport was reinstated.

In 1983 Cunard Line acquired Norwegian American Cruise Lines' two vessels, *Vistafjord* and *Sagafjord*. This brought the Cunard passenger fleet up to five ships and gave them a foothold into the German market, where NAC was popular. These elegant vessels offered 5*+ cruising. Cunard retained their Norwegian crews and the ships' names, changing only their livery.

In October 1986, when *QE2* was close on twenty years old, she underwent a major six-month refit at the Lloyd Werft yard in Bremerhaven, underlining Cunard's commitment to maintaining a transatlantic liner service into the twenty-first century. The decisions leading up to this £100 million investment boiled down to two main options – run the ship to the end of her useful life and scrap her or completely refit and upgrade her. A third option to build a replacement was rejected as totally unsustainable at that time. The costliest part of the upgrade was installing new diesel-electric engines, combined with new variable-pitch propellers. It was projected that this would cut fuel costs by 50 per cent.

On her post-refit sea trials, *QE2* officially maintained 33.1 knots; unofficially she exceeded 34 knots. Her service speed was 28.4 knots, with an additional four knots in hand in the event of delays. Even in full reverse she could manage 19 knots, leading to the comment, when sailing in tandem with *Queen Victoria* to New York in her final season, that *QE2* could keep up with her sister even if sailing backwards!

In addition to the new engines, there were substantial renovations to the interiors. An arcade of shops was installed in the upper level of the Grand Lounge, where once had been seating. The forward observation bar became part of the galley and the tourist-class library was made into a casino and bar. Additional staterooms were built on Signal Deck forward of the funnel, while others were redecorated and all were supplied with

televisions. Despite the work overrunning and some facilities not being available on her maiden voyage as a diesel-electric ship, most people enjoyed the revitalised vessel.

To celebrate her return to service, a party was thrown on *QE2* for 500 underprivileged children from Southampton, with guest of honour HRH Diana, Princess of Wales. The day was topped off with a flypast over the world's most famous ship by, arguably the world's most famous plane, Concorde.

After her major refit in 1993, entitled 'Project Lifestyle', *QE2* arrived back in Southampton. In order to test her stability after the immense structural work undertaken, the ship went to the container terminal, where a number of 20-foot tanks full of water were placed on her decks. (Andrew Sassoli-Walker)

By 1993 Cunard offered a variety of cruise experiences; *Queen Elizabeth 2* remained the flagship. *Sea Goddess I* and *Sea Goddess II*, acquired in August 1986 on a twelve-year charter, were more akin to private yachts, with 116 passengers and eighty crew, operating imaginative itineraries with all-inclusive service. The classic *Sagafjord* and *Vistafjord* catered for experienced cruisers in an ultra-deluxe setting while following a joint venture with Crown Cruise Line, *Cunard Countess* and *Cunard Princess* were joined by *Crown Dynasty*, *Crown Monarch* and *Crown Jewel*, all of which offered an informal style with port-a-day cruises in the Canaries, Mediterranean or Caribbean.

In 1996, after substantial losses, the Norwegian corporation Kværner acquired Trafalgar House, and put Cunard on the market. Unable to find a buyer, they instead made substantial investments to turn the company around. *Sagafjord* was sold in 1997 and two years later *Vistafjord* was renamed *Caronia*, staying with Cunard for another four years before joining her sister ship in the Saga Cruises fleet. In 1998, Carnival Corporation acquired 68 per cent of Cunard, buying the remaining stock the following year.

In 2008 the news broke that *QE2* was to be sold. Her final voyage sold out in minutes, such was the affection held for this unique vessel. At the end of her working life, *QE2* had sailed over 5 million nautical miles, carried over 2.5 million passengers, completed twenty-six world cruises and crossed the Atlantic 803 times.

Perhaps the last word on her should go to her final master, Captain Ian McNaught:

QE2; what can I say; being with her was like being married; it had its ups and downs, but you knew she was something special and yes, I loved her to bits.

Of course she was not everybody's cup of tea when she first came out; she was radically different from the old Queens – 'Ships have been boring too long' was the slogan. She was very much a ship of the sixties; her only competition at the time on the Atlantic was the beautiful *France*, but the British had been brave, and you had *Oriana* (1950), *Canberra* (1961) and *QE2*, all fantastic demonstrations of British ingenuity and huge leaps forward from the traditional ships built after just the Second World War.

I can remember as a schoolboy watching the launching on the television, and already wanting to go to sea, something I had inherited from my father. I was fascinated by her; here was something modern, something of its time, something different.

I did not join her until 1987, after some sixteen years at sea and immediately after the re-engine project, and to more controversy, just like in the beginning. This time it wasn't turbine problems, this time it was Grimm Wheels falling off, and the ship not being ready for passengers, and I can remember seeing a picture of Captain Portet in one of the newspapers, with a really disparaging article about the ship and thinking, have I done the right thing?

Once I joined, I never had any doubts. Yes she had problems, but she just enveloped you and drew you in and you became part of something greater than yourself.

Transatlantic crossings were fantastic, this four-day dash across the ocean at twenty-nine knots, a voyage with real purpose, no matter what the weather. The ship just took on this four-day routine to entertain the passengers, Captain's receptions, cabin parties, church service on Sunday mornings, black tie dinners, afternoon tea served by waiters with white gloves, and lectures from some of the biggest names around at the time; the ship did not need the outside world for those four days, it was like magic, and before you knew it, you were berthing in Pier 90, Manhattan.

The world cruise was something totally different again. After Christmas in the Caribbean the ship would transform itself with a new atmosphere, with passengers on board until the end of April for this leisurely

Above left: In 1993 Cunard entered a joint venture with Crown Cruise Line. One of their three ships was *Crown Dynasty*, seen here in Southampton alongside *QE2*. *Crown Dynasty* is now Fred Olsen's *Braemar*. (Andrew Sassoli-Walker)

Left: Although in the twilight of her career, *QE2* still made for a majestic sight throughout her final voyages in autumn 2008. (Andrew Sassoli-Walker)

Above: *Caronia* at Venice in her final season with Cunard before joining Saga Cruises as *Saga Ruby* in November 2003. (Sharon Poole)

Opposite page top left: Passengers watch as *QE2* receives a fireboat salute on her final call at Getxo for Bilbao on 24 October 2008. (Sharon Poole)

Opposite page bottom left: In her farewell year of 2008, *QE2* met up with her fleet sisters for their final time together in their home port of Southampton. Cunard term this a Royal Rendezvous. (Andrew Sassoli-Walker)

Above right: QM2 steams past QE2. (Andrew Sassoli-Walker)

Right: The foaming wake is the only sign of progress as QE2 steams across the North Atlantic in 2006. (Sharon Poole)

circumnavigation of the world. Everybody knew everybody, passengers would book the same cabin year after year, and the whole ship just relaxed and enjoyed itself. How could you not? As well as all the small ports you had three days in Hong Kong, three days in Sydney, and fantastic tours for passengers like safaris in Kenya, Agra in India, the Great Wall of China, just to name a few.

However it was not all about passengers. The heart and soul of the ship was the ship's company, and it was these 1,020 people who made her what she was; it was they who gave the ship her character. To some passengers I don't think it mattered where *QE2* was, they had come to enjoy the ship and the crew. We had a very close relationship with our passengers, and I think some of the more modern larger tonnage must miss out on this aspect. There were still many crew members who, when we took her to Dubai in 2008, had been there since the maiden voyage, virtually forty years of service in one ship. I can remember one restaurant manager who only had three ships in his discharge book, *Queen Mary*, *Queen Elizabeth* and *QE2*. The loyalty to *QE2* was enormous, and you cannot buy that, or pretend, it was real and tangible, and it did not matter what your job was in the ship, you were part of something special.

There are many special memories for me, I suppose the first time you take command is a unique day; all of a sudden it is all yours, and everybody is looking at you to provide order and direction; this is what you have worked for all your life – to be in command of the most famous ship in the world. Sailing out of Southampton that day, and having cleared Nab Tower and set speed for New York, to come down from the bridge into the captain's quarters for my supper just made me feel very humble, but proud, and to be honest, a little nervous, the beginning of a great adventure.

In 2007 we had a cruise around the UK to celebrate her fortieth anniversary since launching on the Clyde, and I had great thrill of taking her to the River Tyne, my home port. As we came up from Southampton

the weather just got worse and worse, until we arrived off the Tyne in black skies, driving rain and strong winds. "Sorry we are not going in," I said. I could see that the locals had turned out in their thousands, but it was a tidal river for us, being so deep, so we only had a short window to make it in. Well we went round three times off the entrance until on the fourth time round, you could see blue sky up-river and the evening sun appearing and the wind beginning to drop, so in we went. I shall never forget that welcome. Thousands had waited so patiently in the wind and the rain to see her come in and to be able to bring my ship home made me feel quite humble and proud.

We also had the honour of entertaining HM the Queen on board in June of that year; she toured the ship and met crew members and passengers, and enjoyed lunch in the Caronia Restaurant, and for me to be the host on behalf of the ship's company was great honour. It became very obvious as we toured the ship that Her Majesty has a huge affection for, and understanding of, ships. One of the highlights was when we went onto the bridge wing and *Queen Mary 2* was in further up river, and we asked if she would blow our ship's whistle in return to the salute from *QM2*, which she enjoyed doing, but what really made my day was her comments about the design of modern ships. However, what she said will remain private between us!

The last royal visit was by HRH the Duke of Edinburgh on 11 November 2008, the day of the final call in Southampton before we sailed to Dubai. What a day that was! The duke, a sailor himself of course, enjoyed his visit and lunched in the Princess Grill. Very soon it was time for departure and the city of Southampton did us proud – fantastic fireworks, music, crowds on the shore all the way down river and hundreds of small boats around us, I don't think there was anybody who did not shed a tear that evening, a sad but glorious celebration of the ship and her long relationship with the port of Southampton.

Above: As *QM2* leaves for a refit in Hamburg on 22 October 2008, she passes *QE2* for the very last time. (Andrew Sassoli-Walker)

Above right: Captain Ian McNaught on the port bridge wing of *QE2* in July 2007. (Ian McNaught)

Right: Captain Ian McNaught shows HM the Queen around *QE2* as she paid a farewell visit to the ship on 2 June 2008. The tour was followed by a reception and lunch on board, at which former Prime Minister Margaret Thatcher and nine ex-*QE2* captains were present, including Captain Peter Jackson, who took the ship to the Falklands in 1982. (Ian McNaught)

Above left: QE2's last arrival at Southampton, 11 November 2008. Early in the morning Caryll Young noticed the Southampton tugs sailing down the estuary: 'I wondered where they were going, but then I heard on the radio that QE2 was fast on the Brambles sandbank. It seemed like she didn't want to come back and finish her long career but the tugs did their work and it wasn't long before I saw her rounding Calshot as she made her way down Southampton Water to her berth.' (Caryll Young)

Left: A scene that was a part of Southampton for four decades – QE2 at her home berth of 38/9 for the very last time on 11 November 2008. (Andrew Sassoli-Walker)

Above: QE2's paying-off pennant flying as she embarked passengers for the final voyage. At one foot for every year in service, this was 40 feet long. (Andrew Sassoli-Walker)

Above left: The date of *QE2*'s last voyage, 11 November 2008, was also Armistice Day. To mark this poignant date, two historic aircraft from the Army Air Corps Historic Flight, a De Havilland Beaver and an Auster AOP, performed a flypast and dropped a million poppies over the ship. (Andrew Sassoli-Walker)

Below left: A Royal Air Force Harrier GR7 of 1(F) Squadron salutes *QE2* with a bow while in the hover – two classic pieces of British history now gone. (Andrew Sassoli-Walker)

Above right: *QE2*'s final departure couldn't have been anything other than spectacular! (Donna Cooke)

Below right: The City of Southampton's final view of the *QE2*. (Andrew Sassoli-Walker)

Only days later we arrived in Dubai on 26 November, with a wonderful arrival salute from HMS *Lancaster*, who manned the side to salute *QE2*, the only time that has ever been done for a merchant ship.

The next day passengers disembarked and we handed the ship over to her new owners at a formal ceremony on the bridge where the Cunard House Flag, our paying off pennant and Red Ensign were lowered for the last time, and the flags of Dubai and Nakheel, the new owners, were raised, I have to say for me, and the other officers on the bridge, the Staff Captain, the Chief Engineer and the Hotel Manager, that was one of the most painful and heart-breaking moments of our lives. It really brought home that *QE2* was gone, and no matter what they did to her thereafter, she would not be the *QE2* we had known and loved all those years.

The modern ships have changed now to satisfy a new market, and we will never see the likes of her again. She is still sadly missed by all who sailed in her, both passengers and crew.

Above left: Captain Ian McNaught watches from the bridge wing as *QE2* arrives in Dubai to an arrival salute from HMS *Lancaster*, the only time that has ever been done for a merchant ship. (Ian McNaught)

Above right: The final log entry for *QE2* as a Cunard liner. (Ian McNaught)

Chapter 2

CUNARD AT THE HEART OF NATIONAL EVENTS

Cunard ships were frequently the focus of major national events. These included a Review of the Fleet at Spithead for the 1977 Queen's Silver Jubilee, the fiftieth anniversary of D-Day and the 200th anniversary of Trafalgar. On 27 July 1990 HM the Queen joined *QE2* at Spithead to mark the 150th anniversary of the first mail voyage of *Britannia*. After unveiling a plaque, she remained on board while the ship sailed back into Southampton – the only time the Queen sailed on *QE2*.

The 150th anniversary of Cunard was celebrated in 1990 with a number of events in Southampton, including a Royal Review of various Cunard vessels including *QE2*, *Vistafjord* and ACL's *Atlantic Conveyor*. (Andrew Sassoli-Walker)

Above left: The fiftieth anniversary of D-Day in 1994 saw major events in both the UK and France. In the Solent, two iconic vessels of their age, *QE2* and P&O's *Canberra*, took centre stage, hosting veterans at the centre of a large naval review. (Andrew Cooke)

Below left: The 175th anniversary of the British Sailors' Society in 1993 was marked with a visit by HM the Queen to Southampton on board HMY *Britannia*. A review of the ships in port was conducted, with *QE2* at her home berth at the QEII Terminal. (Andrew Sassoli-Walker)

Above: To commemorate the fiftieth anniversary of D-Day, a major event was held in the Solent with naval and merchant vessels assembling for a review by HM the Queen. *QE2* and *Vistafjord* were both there for this historic event. (Andrew Sassoli-Walker)

Above and below left: *QE2* was centre stage in Plymouth Sound as part of the commemorations marking the fiftieth anniversary of VE Day on 3 May 1995. It was her first visit to the Devon city. (Andrew Sassoli-Walker)

Above: Another Spithead review in the Solent, this time marking the 200th anniversary of the Battle of Trafalgar, 28 June 2005. *QE2* took part as well as naval and merchant vessels from many nations. (Andrew Sassoli-Walker)

Opposite: HM the Queen celebrated her Diamond Jubilee in 2012. To celebrate, all three Cunard ships assembled in their home port of Southampton for a host of events. On arrival, all three ships met bow to bow before moving to separate berths. They met again as the day was rounded off with a firework display as the ships set sail. (Andrew Sassoli-Walker)

QM2 arrives at dawn in Southampton for a meeting of the Cunard fleet to mark the Diamond Jubilee of HM Queen Elizabeth in June 2012. (Sharon Poole)

Chapter 3

THE FLEET TODAY

Today Cunard boasts one of the youngest fleets afloat in its three vessels – *Queen Mary 2* (2004), *Queen Victoria* (2007) and *Queen Elizabeth* (2010). Uniquely, every Cunard Queen has been named by a member of the British royal family. On 13 January 2011, all three ships met for the first time. On a snowy day in New York City, *Queen Victoria* was first to arrive, berthing in Manhattan at Pier 88. She was closely followed in by *Queen Elizabeth*, heading for Berth 90. The pair had crossed the North Atlantic in tandem for the previous eight days to rendezvous with *Queen Mary 2*, already at her berth in Brooklyn. As it was *Queen Elizabeth*'s maiden call at NYC, there were a number of official duties to undertake, not least the traditional exchange of plaques. Around 6 p.m. the liners left in the same order they had arrived, to a tumultuous farewell including fireworks and a twenty-one-gun salute as they passed the Statue of Liberty. Since then, they have met a number of times, but perhaps the most memorable was on 4 June 2012 to mark the golden jubilee of HM the Queen in Southampton.

QUEEN MARY 2

Since launch, *Queen Mary 2* (QM2) has remained unchallenged as the world's largest, longest, tallest, widest and most expensive ocean liner ever built. In her first ten years of service she has sailed the equivalent of three times to the moon and back and carried over 1.3 million passengers. In 1998, when Carnival Corporation & plc purchased Cunard from Norwegian shipbuilders Kvaerner ASA, Micky Arison, then CEO of Carnival Corp, set about returning Cunard to its niche position in the market. They disposed of the smaller cruise ships and, in an audacious move, authorised the building of a new transatlantic liner, a type of vessel no-one thought would ever be built again. Uniquely, *QM2* was conceived from the outset as an ocean liner rather than a standard cruise ship, resulting in the new ship costing more than any ship ever built, since a specialised design would be required, able to withstand the worst the Atlantic could throw at her and still maintain a regular schedule.

Above left: On 13 January 2011, *QM2*, *Queen Victoria* and *Queen Elizabeth* met in New York Harbour for a Cunard Royal Rendezvous, marking *Queen Elizabeth*'s maiden call at the city. All three vessels gathered at the Statue of Liberty for a spectacular fireworks display by world record holders, Grucci. (Cunard © Jonathan Atkin)

Above right: The current Cunard fleet of *QM2*, *Queen Elizabeth* and *Queen Victoria* in their home port of Southampton in July 2012. (Fay Jordan)

Opposite page: Dr Stephen Payne, pictured on *QE2* leaving New York, with the Verrazano Narrows Bridge in the background. (Stephen Payne)

Enter Stephen Payne OBE RDI. At the age of twelve he read an article in the 1972 annual produced by the BBC children's programme *Blue Peter* about the demise of the original *Queen Elizabeth*, which claimed that nothing like her would ever be built again. Stephen wrote to *Blue Peter* saying that when he grew up his dream was to be the designer of a transatlantic liner and wanted to prove them wrong. He received a reply advising him not to be disappointed if he didn't realise his ambition and a blue *Blue Peter* badge, a gift to all children who are mentioned on the programme.

Stephen maintained his desire to become a marine architect through to university, when he was advised by a number of people to change direction to chemistry, a degree with better job prospects. After a year studying chemistry, he met up with a former master who said he should follow his dream and went on to help Stephen change his course to a degree in Ship Science (naval architecture) at the University of Southampton.

On graduating Stephen started work for Marconi Radar. However, one of the many companies Stephen had contacted, Technical Marine Planning

Ltd (later part of the Carnival Group), offered him the opportunity to join them as a junior naval architect. After assisting with various projects, he was put in charge of designing and project-managing the new flagship for Holland America Line, *Rotterdam VI*.

While Stephen was mid-Atlantic on *QE2* in 2000, the news broke that Carnival had bought Cunard and they planned to build a new transatlantic liner. Initially they approached major shipyards for speculative designs but they were not suitable for the kind of service Cunard had in mind, so an in-house team was assembled to bring the project to fruition. Until then Stephen had been designing and building ships exclusively for cruising but this was an altogether different proposal. For starters, the thickness of the steel plating in the hull had to be more than twice as thick as normally used to enable the ship to withstand the worst possible weather on the Atlantic. This, together with other unique requirements, led to the design working out at approximately 40 per cent more expensive than an equivalent cruise ship. To justify the cost, Stephen showed photographs of damage inflicted to *QE2*, when hit by a huge wave during a transatlantic crossing. Commodore Warwick remembers such an event in 1995:

After clearing Bishops Rock early on the morning of 8 September 1995, a great circle course was set for New York. During the passage the weather situation for the whole of the Atlantic is monitored regularly and accordingly the movement of Hurricane Luis was being plotted since the voyage began. As the hurricane left the Caribbean it became apparent there was a chance it would pass close to the course of the *QE2*.

On 10 September the great circle course was abandoned and altered to south-westerly to increase the distance from the predicted path of the storm. In the morning speech to passengers, I informed them of the proximity of 'Luis'. At the same the crew prepared for unfavourable weather conditions.

By the time dinner was over, the winds had strengthened to more than fifty knots, far greater than anticipated, and despite the storm being more than 140 miles away the wind speed was recorded at well over 100 knots, causing the ship to list seven degrees when it was on the port beam. By this time 'Luis' was making a forward speed estimated to be between 40 and 50 knots. As it headed north-easterly, the wind soon started to move from the port beam to the bow and we began to encounter very heavy head seas. It became necessary to reduce speed and by early Monday morning *QE2* was hove to and riding out thirty- to forty-foot waves. At 02:10 a rogue wave was sighted right ahead, looming out of the darkness, and it looked as though we were heading straight for the white cliffs of Dover. The wave seemed to take ages to reach us, but it was probably less than a minute before it broke with tremendous force over the bow of *QE2*. An incredible shudder went through the ship, followed a few moments later by two smaller shudders. At the same time the sea cascaded all over the fore-part of the ship, including the bridge, and it was several seconds before the water had drained away from the wheelhouse windows and vision was restored.

QE2 withstood the severity of the impact and the weight of hundreds of tons of water landing on the bow. There was some superficial damage such as bent railings and buckled deck plating but nothing that would not be reasonable to expect under such circumstances. No passengers or crew were injured. The presence of the wave was recorded by Canadian weather buoys moored in the vicinity which measured the height as 98 feet. In my thirty-eight years at sea this was the largest wave that I have ever encountered and I cannot begin to imagine what effect it would have had on a smaller vessel – all I can say is that I was glad that I was on board *QE2*!

Originally, it was assumed the new ship would take over *QE2*'s voyages. This would restrict her beam so she could transit the Panama Canal. This posed a financial conundrum in how to ensure the necessary profit was

made from the ship to justify the build costs. Stephen convinced the Carnival Board that reducing the size of the ship for one transit per year was not worth it. As ships become larger, the price per passenger per berth decreases; this is the 'economy of scale' argument. To justify the additional cost, the new ship would have to take full advantage of this effect.

QE2 had an aluminium superstructure which became brittle in her later years so Stephen designed the new vessel to be totally built of steel. If the ship had been restricted to Panamax dimensions, the additional weight of

The aluminium superstructure of *QE2* became somewhat brittle in her later years, one reason why steel was chosen for the entire hull of *QM2*. (Sharon Poole)

steel in place of aluminium would have resulted in the new vessel being one deck less than *QE2* for stability reasons, and in consequence smaller and once again not commercially viable.

There were three other dimensional constraints: the ship could not be longer than the swinging ground of her UK home port of Southampton, this being the turning circle off the berth; she had to clear the Verrazano Narrows Bridge over the Hudson River at the entrance into New York and she had to offer passengers at least the same amount of balconies as a standard cruise ship. The problem with the latter was how to protect them from North Atlantic storms. It was resolved by positioning the lower deck balcony staterooms within the internal hull and above the two main decks of public rooms. These balconies therefore have a steel bulwark rather than the more usual glass wall protecting them from errant waves and providing shelter from the wind.

The profile of the ship is what Stephen describes as 'the classic pyramid liner shape'. This design ensures an even weight distribution matched to buoyancy, crucially important during heavy transatlantic weather, where a ship will bend and twist if these parameters are not properly matched.

There had to be significant installed power, not only to enable crossings of the Atlantic at high speed, but also for the huge demands on the hotel side. To save weight, the shipyard recommended four diesel engines low down in the hull, with two gas turbines located up behind the funnel; these are all connected to electrical generators. This configuration allows flexibility for the ship to run at slower speeds while cruising and higher speeds transatlantic, while still supplying sufficient power for the facilities on board. Instead of traditional propellers and rudder, four Rolls-Royce Mermaid propulsion pods were used. Each pod contains an electric motor that powers each propeller and pulls rather than pushes the vessel through the water. These have the advantage of offering around 7 per cent greater hydrodynamic efficiency; no rudders

Top: QM2 just clears the Verrazano Narrows Bridge at the entrance to the Hudson River and New York harbour. The height of the vessel's funnel was restricted by the necessity to sail under this bridge. (Howard Paulman)

Below: QE2 bore the label of the last transatlantic liner for so long that *QM2* is the ship many thought would never be built. (Andrew Sassoli-Walker)

QM2 departing Southampton on 8 June 2013. Her profile is what marine architect Dr Stephen Payne calls 'the classic pyramid liner shape'. (Sharon Poole)

As the sun rises over Southampton Water, the unmistakable profile of *QM2* is seen passing the historic Hythe Pier after another transatlantic crossing in 2014. (Andrew Sassoli-Walker)

or stern thrusters are required and thus less maintenance; and there is a quieter experience as there are no long propeller shafts and A brackets to locally disturb the water flow, a common cause of vibration in aft areas of ships. This makes *QM2* the first four-propeller ocean liner since *France* of 1962 and is illustrative of the power required to cross the North Atlantic while maintaining a schedule. The two forward pods are positioned away from the centreline of the ship and are fixed, providing only forward and reverse power. The two aft pods are fully rotational and provide both power and steering. Three bow thrusters provide additional manoeuvring capability in port. Four stabilisers, each 15 feet in length, counteract roll in high seas.

At Stephen's side throughout the design process was Gerry Ellis, Cunard's first new-build director for twenty-five years, and together they headed up a large team of specialists. Where Stephen brought expertise in the design of ships, Gerry brought his experience as a deck officer, particularly important in the layout of the bridge and other operational areas. The entire design of *QM2* is an evolution of the very best of transatlantic liners of yesteryear, combined with state-of-the-art facilities for both passengers and crew.

Of the five European shipyards invited to tender for the build, three dropped out, leaving just Chantiers de l'Atlantique of St Nazaire and Harland & Wolff of Belfast.

Although enthusiastic and capable, Harland & Wolff couldn't match the financial guarantees of the French with the backing of their large parent, Alstom Group, and so it was Chantiers de l'Atlantique, builders of two of the most beautiful transatlantic liners, *Normandie* (1935) and *France* (1962), who secured the contract.

Commonly known as the 'captain's cufflinks', the spare blades for *QM2*'s pods are attractively displayed like works of art on the fore deck. (Andrew Sassoli-Walker)

Above: QM2 under construction at the Chantiers de l'Atlantique shipyard in St Nazaire, France. (Vitor Francisco)

Right: Commodore Ron Warwick with his new command, *QM2*, under construction at St Nazaire. (Ron Warwick)

Opposite page: Clearly illustrating *QM2*'s evolution from liners of the past – the bow, V-shaped breakwater and curved front superstructure take inspiration from the *QE2, Normandie* and the original *Queen Mary* respectively. (Andrew Sassoli-Walker)

The superlatives of *QM2* are too many to mention, such is the uniqueness of the vessel. The mast has a design feature, also used on *QE2*, which is probably unnoticed. In calm conditions, the flags flown from the mast – the Red Ensign, Cunard house flag, courtesy flag of the country where the ship is berthed and any other signal flags – may lie limp. However, by having air conditioning exhaust vents in the mast, the Red Ensign always dances as if in a wind!

Stephen would have preferred a taller funnel, but due to the height restrictions of the Verrazano Narrows Bridge, it is comparatively stumpy. Even so, at high tide there is less than 3 metres of clearance between the top of the funnel and the bridge. Stephen's favourite ruse when sailing on *QM2* is to shout 'duck' as the funnel approaches the bridge, as the perspective always conspires to give the impression that the two will collide! He added, 'passengers rarely fail to respond by crouching down!' A tall funnel disperses smoke further from the aft passenger areas, whereas a smaller funnel can be problematic, with smoke leaving the funnel and rolling downwards. However, using the

Left: Oops! The Red Ensign flies upside-down as *QM2* sets sail on an Eastbound crossing to New York. (Mark Thomas)

Opposite page left: Bridge wing of *QM2*, clearly showing the 4-metre extension to improve visibility down the length of the ship. (Stuart McGregor)

Opposite page top right: *QM2* departing from the QEII Terminal in Southampton, showing the improved visibility from the larger bridge wings. (Andrew Sassoli-Walker)

Opposite page bottom right: *QM2*'s funnel is an effective aerodynamic design, with the huge wind scoops ensuring any soot is blown clear of the aft decks. Two of her four whistles are seen here, the others being on the mast and the bow. The starboard one is from the original *Queen Mary*, while the port whistle is a modern replica. (Andrew Sassoli-Walker)

wind scoop design from *QE2*, air is forced up from the base, pushing any smoke higher as it leaves the funnel. The funnel also incorporates two whistles, one taken from the first *Queen Mary*. This was originally steam powered but as no high-pressure steam is available on *QM2*, it was modified to use compressed air. On the ships of yesteryear there would also be a large discharge of steam as the whistle sounded, so with further attention to detail, Stephen ensured that a small steam line was placed inside the whistle to recreate the effect when the whistle sounds. It is pitched two octaves below middle A – the same as *Mauretania* and *Queen Mary*! Such is the continuity that runs in a great line such as Cunard.

The bridge wings are enclosed to protect the sensitive electronic manoeuvring systems from the elements. The bridge was initially designed to be 45 metres wide but was later increased by a further 4 metres each side to improve visibility aft along the length of the ship for docking manoeuvres.

With the enormous forces of numerous crossings of the Atlantic, Stephen was determined that the structural strength of the ship had to be maintained so the internal layout had certain fixed areas that the interior designers had to work with.

One of the most memorable rooms on *QE2* was the Queens Room, a large ballroom for hosting the cocktail parties and dances for which Cunard are renowned. There is, naturally, a Queens Room on *QM2*. Here daily dance lessons are held on sea days while in the evening, guests may show off their newly-learned steps dancing to the on-board orchestra. Cunard is one of the few lines that carry gentlemen hosts to dance with single female passengers. The Queens Room is also the venue for the famous white-glove afternoon tea.

If there is one area in particular that is reminiscent of the classic liners of the past, it is the Britannia restaurant. Two decks high with a further domed central area, it spans the full width of the ship. This huge space can seat 1,347 people at each of two sittings. There are three other restaurants for higher-grade staterooms – Britannia Club and the Princess and Queens Grills – all offering single-sitting dining.

Out of the 1,310 staterooms, 1,017 are outside, of which 955 have balconies. Across a variety of grades are thirty cabins that are totally accessible to people with disabilities, including full wheelchair access and Braille and tactile signage for visually impaired passengers. Another thirty-six staterooms have been designed specifically for passengers with hearing impairments.

The beautiful Queens Room on *QM2* offers the largest ballroom afloat at 7.5 metres by 13 metres. (Andrew Sassoli-Walker)

Right: The Britannia Restaurant on *QM2* is inspired by the splendid dining rooms on the ocean liners of the 1930s. On the aft bulkhead is a tapestry by Dutch artist Barbara Broekman featuring the original *Queen Mary*, interwoven with the New York skyline seen through a section of Brooklyn Bridge. (Andrew Sassoli-Walker)

Above: There are ten different categories of staterooms, ranging from inside cabins up to the two luxurious Balmoral and Sandringham duplex suites pictured here. At a massive 2,249 square feet over two levels, these feature large balconies overlooking the stern decks, a dining area for eight people, a master bedroom upstairs with 'his and hers' dressing rooms and a guest bathroom and shower downstairs. (Cunard)

Left: The wide expanse of private teak deck available to those who indulge in one of the duplex suites. (Andrew Sassoli-Walker)

Above: A standard outside cabin on Deck 5 of *QM2*. (Andrew Sassoli-Walker)

Opposite page left: HM Queen Elizabeth II names *QM2* at a glittering ceremony in Southampton on 8 January 2004. Also present were Micky Arison of Carnival Corp, Pamela Conover of Cunard and the master of the new ship, Commodore Ronald Warwick. (Cunard)

Opposite page right: Three generations of the Warwick family on *QM2*. (Ron Warwick)

The first steel was cut in January 2002, with the keel laying ceremony held on 4 July 2002, not only Independence Day in the United States but the anniversary of the first scheduled departure of Cunard's paddle-steamer *Britannia* from Liverpool to Halifax in 1840.

Commodore Warwick was her first master and recalls that she handled exceptionally well from the start.

The bridge team significantly benefitted from the ship-simulator training we received in the USA. The initial plan was for the ship to go from St Nazaire straight to Southampton. I, however, felt that it was important to carry out our own trials with the ship's company. I therefore went to Vigo, Spain, a few months before completion and arranged with the harbour authorities and Chamber of Commerce for the ship to visit without any formalities or ceremony. After leaving St Nazaire we sailed directly for Vigo and arrived there the following day. For the next twenty-four hours we carried out an intensive series of tests and routines. The ship was docked several times, mooring arrangements tried out and the gangways rigged. The bow thrusters, stabilisers, lifeboat launching, pontoon rigging and anchors were all tested. Numerous checks and procedure methods of engine room and bridge equipment were carried out. Lifeboat, evacuation

and fire drills were held. Christmas was effectively cancelled because we all had so much to do. However, we managed a Christmas dinner on the way across the Bay of Biscay. However, even this was really a test of the culinary and hotel procedures with dinner being served in the restaurant to all the crew.

After her naming in Southampton by HM Queen Elizabeth II on 8 January 2004, *QM2* prepared to set sail on her maiden voyage. The media were well represented and the children's programme *Blue Peter* sent a film crew to the ship, catching up with Stephen in the Britannia Restaurant, where they interviewed him about the challenges in designing a ship like *QM2*. Stephen was then presented with the programme's highest honour, a gold *Blue Peter* badge to add to the one that he had received in 1973. Stephen says that although he has received many awards, including an OBE, his gold *Blue Peter* badge is very special since so few are awarded each year.

QM2's maiden world cruise took place in 2007, with a celebrated meeting with *QE2* in Sydney. It was *QM2*'s first call at the Australian port and she arrived to a flotilla of yachts, fireboats and small craft. When *QE2* arrived later that evening the event was marked with a gun salute from Fort Denison, followed by fireworks.

Captain Bernard Warner transferred to Cunard Line and was appointed master of *QM2* in 2005. He regards it as the proudest moment of his seagoing career. 'This was the most famous shipping company in the world, operating the iconic ocean liners *QE2* and *Queen Mary 2*. I was also joining a company in expansion, with *Queen Victoria* and *Queen Elizabeth* on the horizon.'

Bernard continues:

Ever since Samuel Cunard first operated liners on the North Atlantic, he had always proclaimed safety before speed. It was therefore gratifying to see that crew members at Cunard were trained to look upon the safety of the ship, her passengers and crew, as a daily necessity entwined into every aspect of shipboard life. Stemming from this safety culture came the creation of a comfortable shipboard environment, in which guests could enjoy the outstanding levels of service, the finest culinary delights and a varied programme of entertainment both by day and by night. Politicians, broadcasters, scientists, explorers, film stars and authors mix with the guests and provide outstanding lectures for the enjoyment of all. Evening shows are every bit as good as those seen in the West End or on Broadway and, once a year, the London Philharmonic Orchestra were always popular guests.

In a fast moving world, Cunard created an atmosphere away from it all, where formality and dressing for dinner became an experience to be relished by the majority of the passengers. Other companies have steadily become more informal but Cunard attracts those who want to recreate those bygone days of elegance.

Cunard does not have any class structure as would have existed in years gone by. Most guests on *QM2* enjoy fine dining in the Britannia Restaurant. The higher-grade staterooms and suites eat in either the Princess or Queens Grill where flambé cooking tableside and a little more personalised service can be expected. Welcome Aboard parties allow the passengers, should they wish, to be formally introduced to the captain and his officers. Giving guests the opportunity to say 'hello' was for me an important part of the voyage.

Throughout the summer *QM2* crosses the Atlantic between Southampton and New York, and there is not a finer or more suitable vessel to fulfil this role. Not only is she spacious and elegant, but she also has the best sea keeping qualities of any other ship on which I served during my forty-five years at sea. The hull of *QM2* is beautifully proportioned to slice through large swells and rough seas with the minimum of fuss.

My love for the sea had been cultivated from boyhood, when I had spent summer holidays sailing and fishing from my father's boat at Sandsend, a picturesque seaside village just a mile or so from Whitby in North Yorkshire. It was therefore a memorable moment when I commanded *QM2* on a circumnavigation of the British Isles and stopped the liner off Whitby harbour in memory of a lifeboatman of the RNLI (Whitby branch) who had recently passed away.

QM2 brings out the crowds in every port she visits around the world, but none more so than in Hamburg, Germany, whose people have a deep affection for the ship. Her citizens line the banks of the River Elbe in their thousands to cheer her arrival and departure from the port every year. But of all the wonderful places the ship visits, St Kitts in the Caribbean was perhaps for me the most inspiring. My ancestor, Captain Thomas Warner, landed there in 1623 from his ship *Marmaduke* and founded the first English settlement in the West Indies. To follow in his footsteps was indeed awesome!

Left: Certificate awarding the Freedom of the City to the officers and crew of *QM2*. (Ron Warwick)

Right: Heavy Atlantic weather on an eastbound crossing on *QM2* in July 2009. (Sharon Poole)

Above left: Commodore Bernard Warner with *QM2* at St Kitts in the Caribbean. His ancestor, Captain Thomas Warner, landed there in 1623 from his ship *Marmaduke* and founded the first English settlement in the West Indies. (Bernard Warner)

Above: Commodore Bernard Warner in April 2011, bringing *QM2* into Southampton on his final arrival before retiring. A water display from the local tugs greeted him and there was a limousine waiting to take him home. (Andrew Sassoli-Walker)

Left: Crowds line the landing stage at Ladungsbrücken in Hamburg as *QM2* departs from Cunard's 'secret home port' on a voyage to Norway in July 2014. The locals have taken the Cunard flagship to their hearts. (Andrew Sassoli-Walker)

Above and below: Celebrating *QM2*'s tenth birthday, all three Cunard ships met in their home port of Southampton for a day of celebrations, culminating in a spectacular firework display. (Andrew Sassoli-Walker)

Top right and right: Near the atrium on *QM2* there are a number of panels representing the four continents of America, Asia, Europe and Africa. On the American one, the artist showed a sense of humour by adding the TV cartoon figure of Homer Simpson watching television! It is very small and unless one knows where to look, it takes quite a while to find it. (Andrew Sassoli-Walker)

I was appointed Commodore (Senior Captain of the Fleet) of Cunard Line in 2007, and in the ensuing years I was privileged to sail with the most professional seafarers and finest ship's company afloat, and indeed have the company of many wonderful passengers from both side of the Atlantic.

QUEEN VICTORIA

In 2003 it was announced that a new ship for Cunard was to be built at the Fincantieri shipyard in Marghera near Venice. The keel of the Vista Class ship was laid down in 2003. It was originally ordered as

Above left: Commodore Bernard Warner next to a painting of his command, the Cunard flagship *QM2*. (Bernard Warner)

Above right: A very special birthday cake, displayed in the Grand Lobby of *QM2* in January 2014, to mark her tenth year in service. (Heather Dove)

Above: *Queen Victoria* arrives at dawn for the Three Queens Event to mark the Diamond Jubilee of Queen Elizabeth II, 5 June 2012. (Sharon Poole)

Above right: A queen and a queen that never was! The bow of *Queen Victoria* and, in the background, P&O Cruises' *Arcadia*, laid down as *Westerdam* for Holland America Line before being allocated to Cunard as *Queen Victoria* and finally going to P&O Cruises as *Arcadia.* (Andrew Sassoli-Walker)

Right: The successful Fincantieri Vista class of cruise ship, adapted to meet the unique requirements of Cunard, resulting in *Queen Victoria* (2007). (Andrew Sassoli-Walker)

Westerdam for Holland America Line but a decision was quickly made by parent company Carnival Corporation & plc to transfer it to Cunard to become *Queen Victoria*. However, changes within the company, combined with a decision by Cunard that the hull should be modified to bring her more in line with *QM2*, saw it transferred to P&O Cruises, becoming the current *Arcadia*. A new vessel was then ordered from Fincantieri for Cunard. This one was 294 metres long (11 metres longer than other Vista Class ships) and 5,000 tons larger, with an additional deck and a strengthened bow to enable her to undertake Atlantic crossings like her sister. Sixty extra cabins were drafted, along with 156 additional balconies. Like *QM2*, *Queen Victoria* has azipod propulsion powered by six Swiss Sulzer diesel engines, and can achieve a maximum speed of 23.7 knots. In addition, three bow thrusters give the vessel unparalleled manoeuvrability and mean that tugs are rarely required in port.

The keel for *Queen Victoria* was laid on 19 May 2005. On 24 August 2007 she sailed out of the Port of Venice to begin her sea trials. Still under the command of the shipyard, these are designed to test engines, thrusters and navigational equipment, as well as establish maximum speed, stopping distances and turning circle. Following successful trials, ownership was officially handed over to Cunard and *Queen Victoria* arrived in Southampton on a cold, crisp morning on 7 December 2007, making fast alongside the City Cruise Terminal in preparation for her naming. The ceremony took place in Southampton on 10 December and was performed by HRH the Duchess of Cornwall, in the presence of HRH the Prince of Wales and over 2,000 invited guests. Unfortunately the bottle of champagne didn't break against the hull at the first attempt, but another was quickly smashed by Cunard officials.

At the time she was the second largest Cunarder ever built, although she is now the smallest of the current fleet. Inspired by liners of the past,

On a frosty December morning in 2007, *Queen Victoria* sails into her home port of Southampton for the first time, greeted by fire tugs and circling helicopters. (Andrew Sassoli-Walker)

Queen Victoria passes P&O Cruises' *Aurora* at the Mayflower Terminal, on her maiden arrival at the City Cruise Terminal in Southampton for her naming ceremony. (Andrew Sassoli-Walker)

Above: The Royal Standard, flying from the mast of *Queen Victoria* on the day of her naming ceremony, 10 December 2007. (Andrew Sassoli-Walker)

Above right: HRH the Duchess of Cornwall, on board for a tour of *Queen Victoria* following her naming in the presence of HRH the Prince of Wales and over 2,000 invited guests on 10 December 2007. (Cunard)

Right: *Queen Victoria* sparkles in the darkness following her naming ceremony in December 2007 before leaving on her maiden voyage the next morning. (Andrew Sassoli-Walker)

some of the decks are higher than usual; the Queens Room, library and shopping area are all two decks high. The décor of the Queens Room reflects Queen Victoria's favourite holiday home of Osborne House on the Isle of Wight, and the shopping arcade is based on the Burlington Arcade in the City of London. The Grand Lobby is three decks high with a staircase reminiscent of the early twentieth-century Olympic Class liners of White Star Line.

The theatre is particularly spectacular and has traditional boxes, just like those in a West End theatre. Other facilities include six restaurants, thirteen bars, casino, card room and three swimming pools. One of the vessel's more interesting rooms is the Winter Garden. Elegantly furnished with cane chairs and tables, and accompanying greenery, it has a magradome or sliding glass roof, so that guests may enjoy sun and fresh air out of any wind.

Left: The magnificent two-deck Britannia Restaurant on *Queen Victoria*. (Andrew Cooke)

Middle: The stairs leading down from the Royal Arcade of shops to the Empire Casino and Golden Lion pub on *Queen Victoria*. (Andrew Cooke)

Right: The Grand Lobby of *Queen Victoria* harks back to the White Star liners of the early twentieth century. The bas-relief of the ship was designed by John McKenna, who was also responsible for a similar artwork on *QM2*. (Andrew Cooke)

Queen Victoria set sail on her maiden voyage on 11 December 2007 and, following a tumultuous send-off, arrived in Rotterdam the following day to a meeting with Cunard's longest-serving liner, *QE2*, leading to a prolonged exchange of whistles.

The following January, she undertook her first world cruise, sailing across the Atlantic in tandem with *QE2*. They arrived in New York to a first meeting with *QM2* – a Cunard Royal Rendezvous of the entire fleet, complete with fireworks, fire tugs and whistles!

The following year, history was made when *Queen Victoria* welcomed Cunard's first female master, Captain Inger Klein Olsen from the Faroe Islands.

QUEEN ELIZABETH

Shortly before *Queen Victoria*'s launch, Cunard signed another contract with Fincantieri to build a sister ship, to be named *Queen Elizabeth*.

The vessel would be a Signature Class vessel, which is a slightly larger, modified version of the Vista Class ships. On 18 September 2008 the first

Above left: The theatre on *Queen Victoria* was the first on a ship to offer boxes, as in theatres ashore. (Sharon Poole)

Above right: Queen Victoria at the City Terminal, before leaving on her first world cruise, in January 2009. (Sharon Poole)

Above left: Captain Inger Olsen, Cunard's first female captain and then master of *Queen Victoria*. (Cunard)

Above right: *Queen Victoria* at the historic terminal at Cherbourg on 23 October 2009. (Sharon Poole)

Below left: The iconic funnel being lifted into place on *Queen Elizabeth*. (Cunard)

steel was cut, with the official keel-laying ceremony on 2 July 2009. When *QE2* retired, Cunard had the youngest fleet in the industry. Although a sister to *Queen Victoria*, *Queen Elizabeth* has a few important differences; her upper decks are longer, giving more space on Lido deck and allowing additional cabins, both achieved by squaring off her stern – a change that easily distinguishes her from *Queen Victoria*. Once again, she has a substantial bow to allow a greater number of crossings in all seasons. The games deck in the forward part of the ship is covered compared with the open version on *Queen Victoria*, and where the Winter Garden on *Queen Victoria* has a sliding roof, the equivalent on *Queen Elizabeth* is the Garden Lounge with a fixed glass roof, the magradome being over one of the pools instead.

The top six Queens Grill suites are named after previous Cunard Commodores, all of whom were awarded knighthoods for war-time services to the Crown, except for Sir Arthur Rostron, master of *Carpathia*, who was honoured for his rescue of *Titanic*'s survivors.

Interiors were designed by Teresa Anderson and show influences of the art deco period in a tribute to her namesake of the 1930s. The centrepiece of the atrium is a 5.6-metre-high marquetry panel of

Above left: The expansive aft deck of *Queen Elizabeth*, pictured on her maiden voyage in October 2010. (Sharon Poole)

Above right: Queen Elizabeth is the newest member of the Cunard fleet and this photograph clearly shows the design differences from *Queen Victoria*. She is seen here passing *QM2* and *Costa Luminosa*, whose design has elements of the original Fincantieri Vista class. (Andrew Sassoli-Walker)

Left: HM Queen Elizabeth II names the newest member of the Cunard fleet, *Queen Elizabeth*, at Southampton on 11 October 2010. (Cunard)

Above: It takes a lot of people to run a cruise liner. Here are the officers and crew of *Queen Elizabeth*, pictured in her maiden season in 2010. (Cunard)

the first *Queen Elizabeth*, designed and made in the Linley workshops using seven different woods, including Madrona, Indian and Macassar ebonies, American and satin walnuts, grey ripple sycamore, burr ash and bird's eye maple. Like her sister, there is a magnificent library which spans two decks, linked by a spiral staircase.

Maintaining Cunard tradition, HM the Queen officially named the ship in a glittering ceremony featuring performances by opera singer Lesley Garrett, the band and pipers of the Coldstream and Scots Guards, plus the Bournemouth Symphony Chorus and Bournemouth Symphony Orchestra conducted by Anthony Inglis.

Such is Cunard's reputation, the maiden voyage sold out in twenty-nine minutes when it went on sale in April 2009, the author (Sharon) being among the lucky ones to secure a cabin. *Queen Elizabeth* set sail on 12 October 2010. After a rousing send-off with a marching band, fire-boat escort and hundreds of smaller craft, she set course for Madeira and the Canary Islands – the same ports of call as *QE2* visited on her maiden voyage back in 1969. At every port there were celebrations, from dancing fireboats at Vigo to a rifle salute at Santa Cruz de Tenerife, as well as the traditional exchanges of plaques with the port agents.

On a beautiful autumn evening, 12 October 2010, *Queen Elizabeth* sails on her maiden voyage. (Andrew Sassoli-Walker)

Above left: Dancing fire tugs provide a display for the passengers on *Queen Elizabeth* on her maiden call, and indeed maiden port, Vigo, in 2010. (Sharon Poole)

Above right: Queen Elizabeth berthed at Lisbon on her maiden voyage in 2010. (Sharon Poole)

At some ports television crews came on board to film the vessel for the local news. Unfortunately, at the final port of Madeira *Queen Elizabeth* was met with torrential rain, causing passengers to be confined on board as the roads began to flood and vehicles were unable to make the dockside. However, that evening surprise guests came on board in the shape of the singers Lulu and Kiki Dee, who performed a concert on board before leaving later that evening.

One distinctive element about Captain Wells' new command was that instead of flying the traditional red ensign of the British Merchant Navy, she flew the blue ensign signifying Captain Wells' commission in the Royal Navy Reserve.

Her maiden world cruise was filled with significant meetings – two Queens in Southampton on departure, three Queens in New York on 13 January 2011, two Queens in Fort Lauderdale and Sydney, *Queen Elizabeth* and *QE2* in Dubai before *QM2* and *QE* arrived back in Southampton on the same day.

Since then, *Queen Elizabeth* has settled comfortably into her role, being based in the Mediterranean for the 2013 and 2014 summer seasons, operating fly cruises. In her first year of service she steamed 123,351 nautical miles and carried 56,049 passengers to 108 different ports from the North Cape of Norway to American Samoa, Los Angeles to Wellington, New Zealand.

In the 1930s, Cunard White Star Line boasted that all twenty-four of their captains were officers in the Royal Navy Reserve, and that twenty-two had Royal decorations. Six were Officers of the Order of the British Empire, two were awarded the Distinguished Service Cross, one was a baronet and one an aide de camp to the king! The tradition continued when Captain Chris Wells took command of *Queen Elizabeth* in 2010, which allowed him to fly the Blue Ensign. (Sharon Poole)

Queen Elizabeth berthed in the Turkish city of Istanbul in 2014. (Marco Sassoli)

Chapter 4

SPRING

In April the ships return to Southampton from their global wanderings and the new season begins.

The bridge is the hub of every vessel. In the early days of steamships, the ship's wheel and steering position was situated on a bridge mounted on top of the two paddle-wheel covers and spanning the full width of the vessel, and thus the origin of the name.

The bridge is the navigation and safety centre of the whole ship and is under the command twenty-four hours a day, seven days a week, of two officers, one of which is a senior officer – either a First or Second Officer – and the other a Third Officer. A system of three watches operates – four hours on and eight hours off. Modern bridge equipment includes a Dynamic Positioning System, which uses sensors to assess wind speed, heading and GPS speed, and will tell officers exactly what combination of thruster and pod power is required to maintain course and position. This is particularly important when docking as it will maintain the bow heading while allowing the captain to move the ship ahead, astern or sideways. As on all modern ships, charts are electronic and are updated weekly. However, for some rarely visited parts of the world, full sets of paper charts are carried as well. Vessels are fitted with Class A Automatic Identification Systems (AIS) which transmit ships' sensor data at intervals so they can be tracked, much like aircraft.

There are no less than five radar scanners on *QM2*; four are forward, covering long range, forward-facing and navigation, and one is positioned at the stern, mainly for use in port for manoeuvring, so the bridge team have 360-degree coverage.

One traditional part of every ship's bridge is the flag locker, which contains the flags of every country the ship is likely to call at, as well as International Code flags. Also called signalling flags, they can be used individually or in combination to convey different meanings. The one seen most frequently is Hotel, which is two vertical halves, one red and one white, and means the ship is under pilotage. Bravo is a solid red flag and is flown when the vessel is refuelling. The flag of the country the ship is visiting is also flown as a courtesy.

Becoming master of a passenger liner is arguably the pinnacle of a mariner's career. Nowadays, the role is closer to that of a chief executive of a small company so diverse is their remit and, reflecting that, becoming a captain is no longer a case of seniority, but of applying for the post and undergoing a rigorous interview and assessment process.

Robert Camby is one of Carnival UK's younger captains. He learned his trade with Princess and Cunard, and was master of *QM2* for a short period in September 2012 before being transferred to P&O Cruises. 'I have a real love for this ship. I fell in love with her within the first ten minutes of being on board back in 2005. I like the Cunard brand, I like the way we have all the cocktail parties and the passenger integration. It is a part of this job that I enjoy.' Juggling the demands of running a ship while maintaining a high profile with the passengers is no easy task. Robert explains, 'The navigational duties always come first. We follow strict hours of work and rest regulations so you must prioritise what is essential

Above left: QM2 entering Southampton Water for the start of another season of ex-UK voyages. (Andrew Sassoli-Walker)

Above right: Captain P. J. Phillpott on the bridge of *Queen Victoria*. (Cunard)

Captain Robert Camby, master of *QM2*, in September 2011. Captain Camby served on board *QM2* from October 2005 until December 2011, rising through the ranks from First Officer, Safety Officer, Chief Officer and Deputy Captain. (Robert Camby)

and what is not. I have a deputy captain who can stand in for me at social events if required so that I can concentrate on the bridge requirements.'

When asked what the favourite part of his role as captain is, Robert's answer is immediate, 'Manoeuvring the ship. That is why we all go to sea as deck officers – aspiring to be captains so we can dock and undock the ships. The safe berthing of a vessel is among one of the most important duties of a ship's captain and he will bear full responsibility if anything should go amiss.'

On the day before, the bridge team will hold a navigational briefing where they plan the arrival, check out charts and note any hazards and check the weather forecast. On cruises, arrivals are usually planned for between 8.00 a.m. and 9.00 a.m. Both captain and deputy captain will be present on the bridge. At 7.30 a.m. 'Stand By Below' is rung to alert the chief engineer that the vessel will be slowing to pick up a pilot and then starting manoeuvring. Approximately fifteen minutes later the pilot is picked up. By then everyone is at their bridge manning positions. A full test of all equipment is carried out and a team briefing held, including the pilot and mooring team. The captain will take control of the ship with the pilot in an advisory role. Following a safe berthing, the pilot will disembark.

Captain Andrew Willard was the first captain seconded to Carnival House as Marine & Nautical Manager. His role included disseminating changes in regulations, marine notifications and safety notices to the fleet and to give a deck department's overview to office-based staff. For example, the French have recently changed the channels off Ushant so that, in an emergency, passenger ships are now within helicopter evacuation range. There is also a shore-based Fleet Captain who joins the ships on a temporary basis to check that best practice is maintained consistently throughout the fleet.

Turnaround day for the great liners of the past took several days to complete, much of which time would be dealing with cargo. All goods for loading had to be delivered to the port within forty-eight hours of sailing. Deck cranes on the fore and aft decks were used to load and off-load cargo.

E. Burnand Mount explained the process in an article contemporary with *Aquitania*. All personnel were paid off at the end of each voyage before going through a process of re-engagement. This included the captain, whose first task on docking was to sign a new contract with the company. Most crew would also sign on immediately for the next voyage as by law, a ship's company had to be maintained at regulation strength. This generated a vast amount of paperwork and had to be completed before Customs clearance could be granted.

The company's Marine Superintendent was in charge of the vessel from the moment the first line was made fast until the last line was cast off. It was his responsibility to handle the paperwork, liaise with various authorities, organise refuelling, taking on of fresh water, repairs and storing to ensure the ship would be self-sufficient for the next six or so days to New York. His office handled the paying off and signing on of crew and the Cunard offices boasted of being able to cope with paperwork for 1,000 men in one hour.

To draw on duty free supplies – spirits and tobacco – from Bonded Warehouses or suppliers, an application had to be made to the Customs authority and once aboard, a Victualling Bill made out. Food and drink were the responsibility of the Chief Steward. He had to calculate what remained from the previous voyage and what was likely to be required on the next one. These estimates would be passed to the Superintendent Caterer, who then arranged deliveries. Meanwhile, the Housekeeping Department would be dealing with a monumental amount of laundry since, although most liners by then had laundries on board, they could not handle the volume of linen used in six days. The Housekeeping Department would take upwards of 100,000 pieces of bed and table linen, towels and crew uniforms and return them freshly laundered within

forty-eight hours. At the same time carpenters and carpet fitters would be inspecting the public rooms and undertaking any necessary repairs. No work was ever done when passengers were on board.

On sailing day, Immigration Department officials would check the papers of all outbound passengers, while the Harbour Master made sure all the port dues were paid. He would agree a time of sailing with the Marine Superintendent and supply tugs. Trinity House was in charge of pilots to navigate the ships through the coastal waters. When everything was complete the Marine Superintendent handed command back to the Captain.

The original Ocean Terminal at Southampton was built in 1911 as the White Star Dock and was the berth from which *Titanic* made her maiden voyage. As other lines began to use it, in 1922 the name was changed to Ocean Dock. At that time it could accommodate five liners; on one such occasion *Mauretania*, *Berengaria*, *Homeric*, *Majestic* and *Olympic* were all in port – some 220,186 grt of shipping! Today it can accommodate just one liner, such has been the growth in size of modern passenger ships. In contrast, however, those five liners had a passenger capacity between them of some 13,124! A staggering amount considering the largest of the ships (*Berengaria*) was 52,101 grt and carried 4,234 passengers, the majority in third class.

Nowadays the two ports that are the busiest for Cunard throughout the year are Southampton in the UK, and New York City, USA. Additionally, during the summer, *Queen Victoria* or *Queen Elizabeth* is positioned in the Mediterranean for fly-cruises and so Venice and Piraeus are also turnaround ports as well as the German city of Hamburg on occasion.

Cunard's links with Southampton date back to 1919, although White Star Line had been based there since 1907. However, it was not until the 1930s that it became their primary port when the introduction of *Queen Mary* and *Queen Elizabeth* required an alternative to Liverpool due to

Left: The iconic Statue of Liberty on the approach to New York, viewed from the deck of *QM2*. (Mark Thomas)

Above: *QM2* arrives early in the morning in Southampton for another turnaround day in winter 2012. (Stuart McGregor)

Opposite page: Over twenty years separates these two images. Summer 1994 – the P&O Containers vessel *Kowloon Bay* (1972), 289 metres long with a capacity of 2,961 TEU (20-foot units), with *QE2* in their home port of Southampton (above). Summer 2014 and *QM2* and *CMA CGM Marco Polo* (2012), at 398 metres long with a capacity of 16,020 TEU (below). The port has spent hundreds of millions of pounds, enlarging terminal facilities and dredging the port and its approaches. (Andrew Sassoli-Walker)

their greater size. Southampton was also conveniently close to Europe and the Port of Cherbourg.

Turn-around day and the two days either side are always the busiest days for the crew. So much has to be organised for a Cunard ship to be turned around in the nine or ten hours she is berthed and everything has to be carried out as effectively and unobtrusively as possible. Within this timeframe, the crew have to offload thousands of pieces of luggage, feed and disembark the passengers from the cruise ending, clean the ship, refuel, remove recyclable materials and rubbish, take on stores, repair or replace equipment, tune all the pianos, be inspected by the Southampton Port Health Authority, prepare the ship for the next passengers, conduct tours of the ship for prospective passengers and travel agents, welcome the new passengers on board, serve lunch, conduct safety drill and many other tasks before another voyage can begin.

When itineraries for the season are confirmed, about eighteen to twelve months earlier, the key factors are available slots for turnaround days since if there is more than one ship in port, everything is multiplied accordingly. Southampton is the number one port for cruise ships in Northern Europe as it is accessible at all states of the tide and has good transport links and easy access to the major tourist destinations of London and Bath. The port has grown over recent years, as has the size of ships, thus needing more stores, fuel supplies and better infrastructure.

Additionally, other shipping has also increased, especially container ships. At the time of writing (summer 2014), a dredging programme is underway to ensure cruise ships and the largest container ships can pass each other at a number of passing points in Southampton Water and the Solent, minimising delays and restrictions on arrival and departure.

Once dates have been secured for turnaround, suppliers are notified of the requirements for each call. Associated British Ports (ABP), the company who run the Port of Southampton, including its four cruise

terminals, will supply a pilot to assist in guiding the ship in and out of port. The captain remains in charge of the vessel, but the pilot has an in-depth knowledge of the location, tidal currents and the effect of the wind and tide on the ship and will be on the bridge in an advisory capacity. Southampton has forty-two pilots who all work on a three-watch shift pattern. Among this group are specialists, otherwise known in the industry as Choice Pilots, who are skilled in large container ships, cruise ships, VLCCs (Very large Crude Carriers), etc. Becoming a Choice Pilot takes at least six years, as each progresses through different sized ships to gain the qualification. Carnival UK, the parent company of Cunard Line among others, has six Choice Pilots.

A Southampton pilot launch, *Hampshire*, returning with the pilot after another departure. (Andrew Sassoli-Walker)

When a pilot is allocated his ship, he produces a passage plan which will detail the tides, weather, other vessel movements and additional information, ensuring safe passage into the port. There are two pilot launches that can take up to eight people from their base in Gosport, Hampshire, out to the eastern entrance to the Solent. The Eastern Pilotage area stretches from the south-east side of the Isle of Wight near Bembridge, at the Nab Tower, as far as the berth. The Nab Tower was one of eight prefabricated towers originally planned as anti-submarine defences during the First World War. They were not all completed in time so in 1920 this one was used to replace a lightship marking a rock at the deep-water entrance to the Eastern Solent. It has a noticeable lean of three degrees, which occurred when it was sunk in position.

The western entrance to the Solent, passing the famous Needles on the western tip of the Isle of Wight, used to be the more popular route as it is shorter, but with shifting sandbanks, it is only used occasionally, if the tide and weather are ideal. If a vessel enters this way, the pilot picks up the ship at West Lepe, which is just north-west of Cowes.

The entrance to Southampton can be tricky. The large amount of traffic using the Solent presents a continual challenge. Additionally, vessels have to negotiate the Brambles sand bank (commonly known in marine circles as the 'precautionary area'). This requires a 110-degree turn, followed by a further 75-degree turn in the opposite direction off Calshot. To assist in the manoeuvre an ABP patrol launch will take station ahead of the ship, ensuring no other craft are within 1 km ahead or 100 metres either side of the ship as she completes the tight turns required in the restricted channel. This is known as a Moving Prohibited Zone.

Throughout the passage, constant radar coverage and monitoring is carried out by Southampton Vessel Traffic Services (VTS), who operate in a similar fashion to an air traffic control tower. At various points along the passage, VTS require the ship to announce her position via radio, which is recorded. As a further safeguard, VTS also offer a countdown in distance as the vessel approaches the 'precautionary area'.

Unless the conditions are particularly bad, the majority of ships arriving and departing do not need the assistance of tugs; most cruise ships today have both bow and stern thrusters and all three Cunarders have azipods, 360-degree rotational propellers.

Cunard ships usually use the Ocean Cruise Terminal (46 Berth) or the Queen Elizabeth II Terminal (38/9 Berth), two of the four cruise terminals available in Southampton. Pilotage time from boarding at the Nab Tower to securing alongside at the berth is approximately two hours.

As the ships come alongside stevedores stand by to secure the ship, while officials are ready to board as soon as the gangway is in position.

Above left: Queen Elizabeth leads *Queen Victoria* and *QM2* into the Solent in July 2012. This image clearly illustrates the sharp turns required off Calshot. (Andrew Sassoli-Walker)

Above right: At dawn, the ABP Port of Southampton patrol launch *SP* heads towards *Queen Elizabeth* ready to escort her through the Solent to the entrance of Southampton Water. (Andrew Sassoli-Walker)

Above left: QM2 towers above the Ocean Terminal in Southampton. (Fay Jordan)

Above right: Mooring deck of the *Queen Elizabeth*. In the past, much of this equipment (cable winches, anchor chains, etc.) was open to the elements on the foredeck. On modern ships it is housed below decks to minimise potential damage from the sea. (Sharon Poole)

These include the ship's agent, UK Border Force (UKBF), Port Health, maintenance personnel, etc. – the list is endless. The ship's house flag and the Red Ensign of the British Merchant Fleet will be raised from the fore-mast and stern jackstaff. As liners the Cunard vessels are never dressed overall with flags, unlike cruise ships.

Once UKBF clear the vessel, disembarkation can begin. The evening before arrival, luggage is collected from outside the staterooms and stored overnight in areas on the lower decks. While passengers enjoy a last breakfast on board, the luggage is taken off the ship on conveyor belts and transported to the terminal, where it is placed in deck order ready for collection. Random checks using sniffer dogs may be carried out to make sure no illegal substances are smuggled into the country. The dogs will also check foodstuffs and goods for delivery to the vessel.

Most passengers disembark via a colour-coded system which takes into account onward travel connections. Southampton's position in the centre of the South Coast means the transport connections to the rest of the

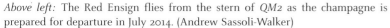

Above left: The Red Ensign flies from the stern of *QM2* as the champagne is prepared for departure in July 2014. (Andrew Sassoli-Walker)

Above middle: The Blue Ensign of the Royal Navy flies from the stern of *QM2*, signifying Captain Christopher Wells' commission in the Royal Naval Reserve. (Andrew Sassoli-Walker)

Above right: Sniffer dogs check out supplies at Ocean Terminal in 2011. (Sharon Poole)

Right: Luggage awaits reclamation at the Ocean Terminal in 2011. (Sharon Poole)

country by air, rail or road are very good and London is only an hour and forty minutes away by road.

By around 10:30 the last passengers will have left the port, so ship visits can commence. These may be for travel agents, to educate them in the Cunard product and fleet, or prospective passengers who want to look over a ship before committing to booking a cruise. Meanwhile, stewards are busy stripping beds, cleaning staterooms, replenishing toiletries and mini-bars, laying out new information folders and generally preparing cabins for the next guests. Contractors may be on board carrying out repairs and a host of other routine or occasional jobs done to maintain the immaculate condition expected of a Cunard liner.

Often there is a change of crew as well as passengers, so transfers to and from airports and the necessary flights will have been arranged for them by Carnival House. A shuttle bus operates between the terminal and the city centre for any crew who have time off during the day.

A bunkering barge arrives shortly after the vessel is alongside to refuel the ship in an operation that can take many hours. Each bunkering barge carries some 2,000 tons of heavy fuel oil. At £50 per ton (at 2014 prices), it is a valuable cargo. The oil is gently heated to ensure it flows through the pipes easily and into the ship's tanks. Under the watchful eye of the Environmental Officer and his team, a waste barge will take recyclable waste to a custom made facility – everything from aluminium, glass, paper and plastics – all of which has been compacted and stored on board until this time.

Southampton Port Health Authority inspects the ships, including public areas as well as behind the scenes in food preparation and storage areas. In such an enclosed space, any form of contamination or bacteria can easily spread. At the US Centers for Disease Control & Prevention (CDC) inspections, Cunard ships regularly score well over 90 per cent.

A bunkering barge alongside *Queen Elizabeth* at the QEII Terminal. It takes several hours to refuel the ship. (Sharon Poole)

Passengers checking in at the Ocean Terminal, Southampton, for a cruise on *QM2* to the Christmas markets of Europe in December 2013. (Sharon Poole)

In the Terminal, check-in staff, mobility attendants and other personnel will be waiting for the first passengers to arrive as embarkation starts around noon. Upon arrival, luggage is taken by porters and placed in a secure area before security scanning. It is then placed in large cages, taken to the dockside and loaded via conveyor belts into the ship. Once on board, the huge task of distributing thousands of pieces of luggage to the correct staterooms begins. Passengers check in before going through the usual scanning procedures prior to boarding.

Throughout the day storing takes place, with lorries bringing everything from steak to toilet rolls. Located deep in the ship, the food storage areas are like a huge supermarket keeping the galleys supplied.

One of the last people to embark in the afternoon is the pilot, to take the vessel out of port in a reverse of the procedure carried out only a few hours previously. The ensigns are taken down, and preparations are made to get the vessel ready for departure. Steering and other systems are all checked. The vessel goes 'To Stations' and 'Stand By Below' is rung to the engine room, while the stevedores stand ready to release the mooring ropes. The pilot radios through to VTS, announcing the departure, confirming draft, number of persons on board, and the destination. VTS will inform the ship of other vessel movements and any information needed for the passage out to sea.

As the ship lifts off the berth, the time-honoured tradition of blowing the ship's whistle three times tells everyone, both on board and ashore, that the voyage has begun! As the vessel sails into the distance, the terminal and port become quiet once more, until this complex operation swings into action all over again the following day.

One European port that has taken Cunard, and *QM2* in particular, to its heart is Hamburg. Commodore Bernard Warner, now retired, had a theory about its popularity. 'I think that *QM2* has this huge affiliation with Hamburg because the Germans would really have liked a new ocean liner of their own. In the past they had *Vaterland*, *Kaiser Wilhelm der Grosse*, *Imperator* and *Bremen* to name a few. Also, Hamburg likes, and does a lot of business with, the British.'

Germany has a seemingly insatiable appetite for the Cunard brand, be it the increasing numbers of passengers every year or the thousands of people that line the historic waterfront along the Elbe, from the Hamburg Cruise Centre, past the jetties at Landungsbrüken to the Fischmarkt at Altona and beyond, every time a Cunard ship visits Germany's biggest port.

Above left: Luggage is brought alongside the ship in wire cages and loaded via conveyor belts onto *QM2*. Then begins the laborious task of delivering it to staterooms. (Sharon Poole)

Above right: Luggage being delivered to staterooms on *QM2* in December 2013. (Sharon Poole)

Above left: Queen Elizabeth departs from the Ocean Terminal on another ex-UK round trip voyage in May 2013. (Andrew Sassoli-Walker)

Above right: The majestic sight of the *Queen Elizabeth* heading towards the Solent. (Andrew Sassoli-Walker)

Germans have been travelling with Cunard for many years, but more especially when Norwegian American Cruises was acquired by Cunard in 1983. Their two ships, *Sagafjord* and *Vistafjord*, had always been popular with Germans and Hamburg was a regular port of call on their Northern European routes.

QM2 first sailed into Hamburg in July 2004, when 100,000 people turned out to witness the event. Since then, Cunard have offered cruises to/from Hamburg on a selection of transatlantic crossings and Northern Europe itineraries. Normally, the ship will sail from Southampton to Hamburg, onto the Norwegian fjords, back to Hamburg, Southampton and then across to New York before returning on an Eastbound crossing to Southampton and Hamburg once more.

Hamburg's Blohm & Voss is also the shipyard of choice for refits, being one of the few who can accommodate *QM2* in what is Europe's largest dry dock (352 metres long).

I (Andrew) recently took the opportunity to visit Hamburg on *QM2*. The ship had over a thousand German passengers who had taken either an eastbound transatlantic crossing or joined for the voyage to Norway. The atmosphere on board was made all the more interesting since the day of departure coincided with Germany playing in the 2014 World Cup final – and winning! After a quiet day at sea, *QM2* glided into Cunard's secret home port, as the company call Hamburg, shortly after sunrise. She swung 180 degrees and berthed in Hafen City. Just before departure that evening, crowds gathered. As the ship made her majestic

In the Hamburg International Maritime Museum is a very impressive model of *QM2*. Made from 780,000 bricks of Lego, it is 6.9 metres long and weighs nearly a tonne! The vessel is depicted in the Blohm & Voss dry dock under refit. (Andrew Sassoli-Walker)

departure, people, both on board and ashore, cheered loudly while Captain Chris Wells made sure it was a memorable send-off, not just with the deep echo of the ship's whistle booming over the Hanseatic city, but with touch of British humour, by playing 'Land of Hope and Glory' over the public address system!

This was a fantastic spectacle to witness and the port and Cunard celebrated their special relationship with a festival on the ship's return visit a few days later.

Above left: A view down the length of *QM2* as she departs Southampton, taken from the forward observation deck immediately under the bridge. (Andrew Sassoli-Walker)

Above right: German passengers celebrate in *QM2*'s G32 nightclub as their team score the winning goal in the 2014 football World Cup. The name was her shipyard number. (Andrew Sassoli-Walker)

Above: In *QM2*'s Illuminations, German passengers get excited as their football team is shown on the large screen playing in the 2014 World Cup. (Andrew Sassoli-Walker)

Above right: Early sunshine bathes *QM2* as she arrives in Hamburg in 2014. (Andrew Sassoli-Walker)

Right: Viewed from the spire of Hauptkirche Sankt Michaelis, *QM2* can be spotted above the rooftops of the rejuvenated old Freeport district, now named Hafen City, in 2014. (Andrew Sassoli-Walker)

Left: Confirming the special relationship between Cunard, *QM2* and the City of Hamburg, a celebration of the ship's tenth anniversary year was marked with a festival in the city in July 2014. (Andrew Sassoli-Walker)

Above: Departing Hamburg in July 2014, *QM2* passes the Blohm & Voss dry dock, where she has been refitted a number of times since 2004. (Andrew Sassoli-Walker)

Chapter 5

SUMMER

Itinerary planning is undertaken by a dedicated team based in Carnival House in Southampton, usually around eighteen months in advance of the brochure launch. To attract both regular passengers and new guests, there will be a mix of popular ports together with some new places – for example Kochi in Japan and Pusan in South Korea for 2015.

A lot of factors are taken into account when deciding where to deploy the fleet – how far is it from the previous port and to the next one, is there a suitable berth or anchorage, are there fuel and fresh water supplies if required, is there enough to attract passengers, sufficient transport for tours, when are the public holidays (meaning some attractions might be closed) and are English and German-speaking guides available? Add in the ever increasing competition for berths from other lines, and the unstable political situation in many parts of the world, and it makes the job of John Heylen, Head of Fleet Operations for Carnival UK, and his team a massive task. Guest surveys also play their part in the planning process – there is no point taking people to a place no one liked! In the last year or so, Cunard has positioned one ship in the Mediterranean, flying passengers out to join her in Italy or Greece. This is ideal for

people with less time or who want to avoid the Bay of Biscay. All these considerations are why it is difficult to find a substitute port at short notice if circumstances force one to be missed, usually due to adverse weather. A decision to omit a port is never taken lightly. Aside from the disappointment caused to guests, there can be substantial costs incurred. Port charges still have to be paid and refunds given to everyone that had tours booked. Additionally, the economy of the destination itself suffers from the loss of passengers' spending money.

Whereas in a liner people travel from A to B, on a cruise it is the itinerary that is the main attraction and, while some are happy staying on board a virtually empty ship and enjoying the facilities, most will be eager to get ashore and explore.

While *QM2* was in the design stage, one of the most important tasks for Newbuilds Director Gerry Ellis was to contact all the ports *QE2* used and check out their suitability for *QM2*, given her much greater size. Where the difficulty was manoeuvrability, then *QM2* would have an advantage, but if it was length of berth or depth of water, then that port would either no longer be viable or they would have to use tenders.

The itinerary planners will try and limit tender ports to no more than two or three per cruise since it is a very intensive day for officers and crew, who have to maintain a regular schedule with the boats and man the tendering pontoons and landing stage. Popular tender ports include Santorini in Greece and the spectacular towns along the Amalfi coast of Italy. The first tender ashore will be crew only. They will assess the area, ensure it is suitable for passengers and set up everything required – safety equipment, radios, canopy to shelter crew and passengers from the sun while waiting, water, etc.

Even when berthing, there is a delay before passengers can go ashore. The gangways have to be safely rigged and clearance given from the port agents, immigration and customs. Security is of vital importance and barriers are erected to prevent anyone approaching the ship without the correct identification. Sadly, gone are the days when friends and relatives could accompany passengers on board to see them off or enjoy a meal together on the ship!

For tour staff, preparations for ports begin immediately the ship sets sail. Numbers for each tour are calculated and final numbers sent to the agents ashore the night before arrival. Despatch sheets are produced and tour stickers printed ready to give out as guests muster for each excursion – this will either be on board in the theatre or ashore on the dockside, depending on the port, weather and the time of the tour.

Passengers have the option to explore independently, book an organised excursion or take a private tour. Cunard tours range from coach drives for those with mobility problems to walking tours or exploring the surrounding countryside. Activity excursions may include cycling, white-water rafting or zip lining through a rain forest.

Whatever passengers choose to do, their day ashore will probably be the hot topic of conversation at dinner that evening.

Above left: Tendering ashore in the Caribbean from *QM2* in December 2013. (Heather Dove)

Above right: *QM2* at the Caribbean island of St Thomas on 26 December 2013. (Heather Dove)

Below: *QM2* with her sister Queen Victoria at Funchal, Madeira, on 8 November 2012. (João Abreu)

Above: *QM2* lies alongside the historic ocean liner terminal at Cherbourg, 2010. (Sharon Poole)

Above right: *QM2* at Flam in Norway, making even those towering mountains seem dwarfed somehow. (Caryll Young)

Right: When *QM2* visited Alesund in Norway for the first time, Caryll Young was on board. She remembers, 'When we sailed, the late afternoon sun cast a glow over the mountains which were capped with snow. There were crowds of people on the waterside and the fireboat was spraying jets of water. Suddenly, from one of the small boats surrounding us we heard our National Anthem being played very loudly, followed by Vera Lynn singing 'We'll meet again' and then the National Anthem again. Perhaps not quite in keeping with the lovely scenery, but it made for a very emotional sailaway.' (Caryll Young)

Above left: A stunning early evening scene with *QM2* berthed below the Akershus Castle at Oslo on 8 November 2013. (Tom Gulbrandsen)

Above right: The funnel of *QM2* just clearing the bridge at Bergen on 29 July 2005. Jean Edwards was on board *QM2* on the ship's first visit to Bergen, Norway. She recalls: 'Due to the tide being high the ship slowed and came to a halt. We were on the seaward side of the great bridge at the entrance to Bergen. As we waited for the tide to drop so that the ship could proceed the passengers were all out and waving to the people on the bridge and in boats around us. Eventually the water dropped sufficiently for *QM2* to move forward. By this time, we were surrounded by fire boats, yachts and small boats. The jets of water from the fire boats made a beautiful display. As we passed under the bridge we could see hundreds of people waving with hands and flags, not only from the bridge, but also from the roads and paths on each side. It was amazing to be part of the procession and receiving such a welcome.' (Tom Gulbrandsen)

Children are well catered for both on crossings and cruises. All the ships have dedicated facilities for youngsters aged up to seventeen, with age-specific activities arranged by the Early Years Staff or Youth Crew. There are three separate areas for different age groups. The Play Zone caters for children up to the age of seven, with play areas, arts and crafts, puzzles and board games. Activities may include scavenger hunts and dancing. The Zone is a permanently staffed sociable area for those aged between eight and twelve (seventeen on *QM2*). The Teen Zone is for the oldest group and is only available on *Queen Victoria* and *Queen Elizabeth*. Activities include sports tournaments, pizza parties and quizzes etc. For teenagers there is also a video games room and lounge area. All are open daily and are free to use.

Summer is a favourite time for weddings. On Sunday 29 April 2012, Denise Holding and Barry Maloney became the first couple to marry on board a modern Cunard ship. The marriage, on *QM2*, followed the re-flagging of the fleet to the Bahamas to enable such ceremonies to take place. Ships are a romantic venue for a wedding, with the added convenience of having everything at hand, from the spa to the on-board florist. A wedding co-ordinator will take care of the arrangements, the galley will make the wedding cake, a room can be reserved for a reception and at the end of the day, the couple will already be at their honeymoon 'resort'. Weddings may only take place on voyages of seven nights or more and, for legal reasons, must take place at sea.

Some of the facilities specifically designed for children on *QM2*. (Cunard)

Chapter 6

AUTUMN

A transatlantic crossing is different from a cruise. It is a journey that, today, can only be undertaken on a Cunard liner, and what better time to visit New England than the autumn or fall. The journey between the Old and New Worlds still carries a sense of embarking on a great adventure. With no ports to interrupt the voyage, passengers slip into a relaxed routine. Once out of sight of the shore and surrounded by a wide expanse of ocean, daily cares seem far away, the passing of time marked only by the sounding of the ship's bell at noon or by the traditional delights of afternoon tea in the Queens Room. 'We are both relishing these days of suspended animation,' wrote Rupert Hart-Davis on the *Queen Mary* in 1961. It is an awe-inspiring sight to be in the middle of the ocean, with not a ship or even aeroplane in sight for days on end, and just the churning wake to provide any sense of progress.

At the Newfoundland Grand Banks the cold Labrador Current mixes with the warm waters of the Gulf Stream. The mixing of these waters and the shape of the ocean bottom lifts nutrients to the surface. These conditions create one of the richest fishing grounds in the world. In summer, they are the feeding grounds of some twenty-two species of whales, including the world's largest population of humpbacks. The same conditions can also cause thick fog. I (Sharon) will never forget the experience of standing on deck on *QE2* as the fog lifted to reveal dozens of whales feeding all around the ship.

As the vessel approaches New York, let Sir Edgar Britten, in command of *Berengaria* in 1936, take up the story for a moment.

Dawn is just breaking now, but already the fairway of the Hudson is black with craft ... Sailing up the Hudson in the old days of the Gedney Channel gave most masters of big ships heart disease, and the bottom of many a vessel has rested comfortably for hours, and sometimes days, on the shoals of Sandy Hook. But with the opening of the Ambrose Channel the river is now one of the most comfortable known to navigation ... It is about six miles in length, 2,000 feet broad, and, cut out of the very centre of the river's bottom, it allows the world's largest vessels to sail right up to the front doors of New Yorkers. The *Lusitania* was the first ship to sail up the fairway in 1907. To my mind it was rather a fine gesture on the part of America to bestow this signal honour on a British ship, for the formal opening of the channel was delayed for two days to await the arrival of the great Cunarder.

Above: The spacious aft decks of *QM2*, with the mesmerising wake marking her course. (Andrew Sassoli-Walker)

Above right: *QM2* in a thick fog bank off Newfoundland. On most transatlantic crossings fog is encountered off the Newfoundland Grand Banks, where the cold Labrador Current mixes with the warm waters of the Gulf Stream. The ship has four whistles – two on the funnel, one on the mast and one on the bow. The forward whistles have a range of ten miles and are sounded a minimum of every two minutes during episodes of restricted visibility. (Sharon Poole)

Right: *QM2* arrives at Red Hook terminal, Brooklyn, as the sun rises over New York City on 1 July 2009. (Sharon Poole)

Such is the regard Cunard was, and is, held in around the world. New York was also Commodore Ron Warwick's favourite port:

Like *QE2*, New York is a symbol of man-made grandeur and achievement. The gateway to the port is under the Verrazano-Narrows suspension bridge - a magnificent feat of engineering named after the Italian explorer Giovanni da Verrazano. This is followed by the Statue of Liberty, Ellis Island and the skyscrapers of Manhattan, all of which tell their own story of America and what it stands for. I think every American should sail into New York at least one in their lifetime.

The Crossing is little different today, although *QM2* takes a more leisurely six or seven days to reach New York from Southampton. In part this is a fuel-saving measure, but allows passengers longer to enjoy the voyage. Nowadays *QM2* normally berths at the Red Hook terminal in Brooklyn rather than Manhattan. Does it get boring for the officers and crew? Clearly not as Commodore Bernard Warner told us:

Although backwards and forwards across the Atlantic during summer may sound monotonous to some, nothing could be further from the truth. The passage route is always different in order to take advantage of the fairest weather, avoid or take advantage of the fast flowing Gulf Stream, and of course avoid the ice, prevalent over the Grand Banks of Newfoundland from February through to late June. The most oft asked question other than "If you're here, who's driving?" was "Will we pass over the wreck of *Titanic*?" We were normally within just a few miles of that fateful position.

Nowadays many cruise lines allow people to bring assistance dogs with them but this is a fairly modern change in line with anti-discrimination laws. Cunard is the only line that continues to regularly carry ordinary

QM2 at her US home port of Red Hook terminal, Brooklyn, New York in July 2009. (Sharon Poole)

QM2 at Red Hook cruise terminal, Brooklyn, with the Lower East Side of New York City in the background. (Sharon Poole)

four-legged guests, although they may only be carried on the non-stop transatlantic crossings between Southampton, Hamburg and New York and must have appropriate documentation. Whereas assistance dogs are allowed to remain with their owners in the staterooms, canine and feline passengers stay in the kennels, located on Deck 12 of *QM2* under the supervision of the Kennel Master. There are six average size kennels and six large ones. Cats require two kennels – one for the animal and one for the litter tray! Dogs are walked every day on an area of deck exclusively reserved for them (*QE2* even had a lamp-post convenience installed when the Duke of Windsor once commented it was a shame the dogs had not got one on their deck!). In case of emergency, the ship carries fifty dog and cat lifejackets in two sizes – which fortunately have not yet had to be used.

Food has always been important to passengers. On most routes there were long days at sea to fill, and meals gave a structure to the day. Cabin passengers ate at one large table in the saloon, over which the captain presided; immigrants travelling third-class would provide and cook their own provisions until the later nineteenth century, when food was included in the ticket price, although not in the quantities and choices served in first-class. Fresh meat soon ran out, leaving salted beef and pork unless the chef killed a chicken or two. Before the days of refrigeration, meat was salted to preserve it, although some ships had cold rooms lined with ice. In 1893 *Campania* and *Lucania* became the first Cunard ships to have refrigerated store rooms. There was frequently a live cow kept on deck to provide milk and hens in wicker cages supplied eggs. Sea air gives people good appetites so meals were long and frequent. It was not unusual to offer a four-course breakfast at 8 a.m., four-course lunch at

The kennel master of *QM2* walks one of his charges. (Cunard)

1.30 p.m. and six-course dinner at 6.30 p.m. In between, there was hot bouillon at 11 a.m. and afternoon tea at 4 p.m. If passengers still felt peckish, hot hors d'oeuvres were served in the smoke-room before bed!

The Cunard Magazine, Vol. 13, No. 6, December 1924, gives an interesting insight into the catering arrangements of the time, as well as a look back to earlier days.

The writer well remembers vessels of the Olympus and Marathon type carrying 100 first class and about 1,000 steerage passengers. The former dined in a saloon on the open deck. It was necessary for the galley, on account of its fires and funnels, to be placed somewhere near the smoke stack, which, in most cases, was a considerable distance away. In fine weather the arrangement worked fairly well, but in the midst of Atlantic storms and freezing winds the passengers were fed under the greatest difficulty … When Mr Guion was building his 'Ocean Greyhounds' … he made better arrangements for the *Oregon*. After making a few voyages under the Guion flag, the vessel was acquired by the Cunard Company. Her new owners were not slow to see the advantage of what had been done in the culinary department, and even improved upon it. A few years later they abolished the ancient gridiron in favour of silver grills … If one is interested in the subject, let him obtain permission to wander round what is in some respects, particularly to ladies, the most interesting part of a big vessel. He will be shown not only huge ranges operated by oil, electricity, or coal, but beautiful grills, roasters, stockpots, bain maries, hot-presses, and all sorts of electrically controlled devices for slicing, mincing, mixing, peeling, triturating, etc. …

Storing *Berengaria* for a single transatlantic voyage in the 1930s involved 12 cwt of tea and the same of coffee, 6 tons of sugar, 500 bottles of sauces, 500 tins of sardines, 250 lbs of caviar, 2 tons of jams and marmalade, 1 ton of dried fruit, 500 tins of biscuits, 12 tons of flour, 1 ton of ham, 2 tons of bacon, 2 tons of butter, 1 ton of cheese, 60,000 eggs, 22 tons of meat, 5 tons of fish, 4,000 chickens and fowl, 250 turkeys, 1,100 pigeons, 700 head of game, 13 cwt sausages, 7 tons of fresh vegetables, 20 tons of potatoes, 35 tons of ice, 1,200 quarts of ice-cream, 1,500 quarts of fresh cream, 2,500 gallons of fresh milk, 12 cwt of grapes, 180 pineapples, 1,100 melons, 1½ tons of tomatoes, 200 boxes each of apples and oranges, 100 boxes grapefruit and 30 bunches of bananas.

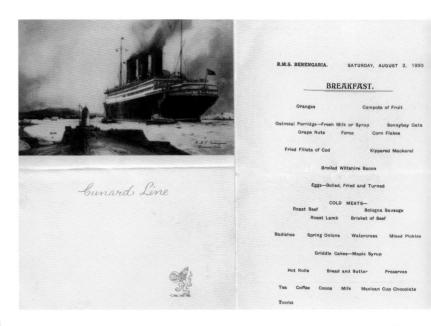

A tourist-class breakfast menu from *Berengaria* on 2 August 1930. Not sure cold roast beef and lamb would go down too well nowadays for breakfast! (Sharon Poole Collection)

Drink included 6,500 bottles of wine, 3,000 bottles of spirits, 260 bottles of liqueurs, 25,000 bottles of beer, 500 gallons of draught lager and 20,000 bottles of mineral waters, although menus carried the warning that the motion of the ship precluded the carrying of older red wines.

Nowadays provisioning is a very smart operation, normally taking around six hours. Years of practice mean stores managers can reliably estimate the amount of goods required, depending on passenger demographics and the itinerary. Before computerised stock control, ships carried sufficient stores for the current cruise plus the following one. This could create wastage so nowadays food and other necessities are only carried for the current cruise, plus a few extra days in case of unavoidable delays.

All food is prepared fresh on board, from the bread rolls at breakfast to the petit fours after dinner. Ingredients are ordered in advance and delivered to the quayside on pallets on turnaround day, loaded onto the ships through the gunports in the sides of the vessels and then delivered to the appropriate storage area using the ship's own fork-lift trucks. Storage rooms are kept at the optimum temperature for their contents – fresh vegetables, meat, fish, etc. Everything is kept spotlessly clean and if rough seas cause any foodstuff to touch the floor, it is written off. Bonded stores hold alcoholic beverages and tobacco.

Cunard's current Global Culinary Ambassador, Jean-Marie Zimmerman, joined the company in 2003.

My initial thought was that this was perhaps just kitchens at sea – a matter of logistics. But as I became absorbed into the history, traditions and innovations of Cunard Line and the Transatlantic Crossing my passion for ocean liners grew. We spend so much time deciding what should be served, how it can be better prepared and how we can make it more attractive to the eye and therefore exciting to the diners' palates.

Preparing afternoon tea in the galley on *Queen Victoria*. (Cunard)

Some of the variety of carved fruit used to decorate Kings Court on *QM2*. (Sharon Poole)

Above left: Just one of the delicious desserts on offer every night at dinner on a Cunard liner. (Sharon Poole)

Above: Rose Warneke with her granddaughters in the Tables of the World restaurant on *QE2*, on a trip to England from New York to visit her family in 1971. Rose was a First World War war bride. (Sharon Poole Collection)

Left: James Thomas holds a sparkler on one of *QE2*'s Gala dinner nights in her farewell year of 2008. Modern Health and Safety regulations would prohibit this nowadays! (Mark Thomas)

Trevor Connelly was the first Carnival UK chef to cross over from P&O Cruises to Cunard, working as Executive Chef on *Queen Elizabeth*. He found that the galleys work on similar principles although some of the ranks are slightly different, with a Chef de Cuisine in charge of the Cunard galleys. Most cruise menus work on a fortnightly cycle with the addition of four gala dinners; world cruises will be slightly different so dishes do not become repetitive. All the menus are worked out by the Development Chef at Carnival House in consultation with the various Executive Chefs as well as Jean-Marie Zimmerman.

In recent months work has been undertaken to modernise Cunard dishes and standardise the Britannia Restaurant menus across the fleet. The whole team are constantly experimenting, for example with healthy lighter meals for the more health-conscious passengers. Dietary chefs are also on board to cater for special requirements such as gluten-free or diabetic meals.

Cunard attract passengers from all over the world and so food is international in style with a British slant. Regional dishes will be cooked if there are large groups of passengers from a single country. When 900 Japanese joined one of the ships in Yokohama for a world cruise sector, a specialist chef was employed and a dedicated breakfast buffet set up to cater for them. Menus can also be translated into foreign languages if required.

The Grills have a separate galley with a greater choice of dishes and 'always available' items. These two restaurants are smaller and more intimate, with a personalised service. They are only accessible to those occupying Princess suites and above. Having said that, some guests on *QM2* who qualify to eat in the Princess or Queens Grill choose to eat in the Britannia Restaurant as it is such a spectacular venue. On *Queen Victoria* and *Queen Elizabeth*, the Grills are in a stunning location high on the ship and overhanging the sides, giving an unparalleled view of the ocean. Between the two grill restaurants is the exclusive Grills Lounge for pre- or post-dinner cocktails. On all the ships a third category of cabin is the Britannia Club Balcony, which allows access to a separate part of the Britannia dining room. The Britannia Club and both Grills offer a single seating for dinner between 18:30 and 21:00, whereas the main restaurant operates two sittings – 18:00 and 20:30.

We cannot leave the subject of food without mention of the famous Cunard white-glove afternoon tea. It is such an institution and so popular that queues form outside the entrance to the Queens Room up to half an hour before serving. Once seated the guest is transported back to a more leisurely period, with a string quartet or harpist playing above the sound of soft chatter and tinkle of spoons against teacups.

The famous Cunard White Glove afternoon tea on *Queen Victoria*. (Solent Richard)

For passengers on the early ships, especially on the North Atlantic route, with little nothing to see but endless ocean, boredom was the greatest problem. They would walk on deck, read or chat with their fellows. In the evenings they would gather in the saloon and tell stories, talk or play cards or chess. Soon they began to organise their own entertainment. On the first day at sea a committee was usually elected, or invited by the purser, to organise games, tournaments and competitions. Gambling and sweepstakes were popular, for example on the distance the ship travelled in one day and, for the more active, deck quoits, with rings of hemp thrown into buckets. As the ships grew larger more space could be devoted to passengers and more amenities provided.

The *Sea Sequel to the Week-end Book* of 1934 provides a whole chapter on games and deck sports played on liners – deck tennis (played with a hemp or rubber ring thrown over a net), shuffleboard, quoits and bullboard (in which you threw rings onto a target or pegs), table-tennis, deck cricket and golf. Those familiar with the netted golf driving ranges on current ships may be amused by the 1934 version:

> There are here and there in the world men who will deliberately tee up no less than twelve balls on the Boat Deck and drive them into the sea. Not many men because it costs something like 2s 6d a drive. An alternative is to buy a sort of captive ball with a parachute attached to it, if you happen not to be rich.

Many of these games are still played today – shuffleboard, deck tennis, and even, on *Queen Elizabeth*, croquet and bowls. On *Queen Victoria* you can take fencing lessons – the first Cunarder to offer them.

In poor weather, indoor pastimes included bingo, card games and horse racing! The latter was played by an officer throwing a dice and metal horses or hobby horses being moved forward the number of paces thrown. Another method was for the horses to be attached by string to a wheel and passengers

Traditional deck sports on a day at sea on *QM2*. (Andrew Sassoli-Walker)

The artificial bowling green on *Queen Elizabeth*, 2010. (Sharon Poole)

taking it in turns to wind the horses in as fast as they could. Nowadays gambling is restricted to bingo or the casino, where guests can while away an hour or two on slot machines or at the blackjack or roulette tables. If you prefer less strenuous days at sea, *QM2* boasts the largest library afloat.

There was usually a fancy dress or masquerade ball, with prizes for the most inventive costume. These were held early in the cruise as a way of getting people together. A remnant of these exist today in Cunard's famous masked balls although I doubt you would be able to procure some of the articles Commodore Sir Edgar Britten lists as available to borrow for costumes – 'From the Officers; Flags, strips of red, white, blue and

There is even a croquet lawn on *Queen Elizabeth*. (Cunard)

The lower level of the duplex library on *Queen Elizabeth*. (Sharon Poole)

yellow bunting; oilskin coats; sou'westers; seaboots; white duck suits; brass buttons; uniform caps; telescope; whistles; revolvers.' Revolvers? Another ice-breaker for passengers came in the form of small cocktail parties and other functions organised by the Staff Captain, Purser and Chief Steward, 'for the purpose of drawing happy groups of passengers together, so that the least timid or shy may not feel out of the fun'. Again – something retained to this day, with the Captain's Welcome Aboard reception and World Club party for returning guests.

In the evenings live music drifts all around the ships, whether it be a harpist playing for cocktails in the Chart Room or a jazz band in the Golden Lion. The Queens Room Orchestra plays every evening for dancing. The band leader liaises with the vocalist to maximise the variety of tunes and dances and to ensure that each dance type is covered, whether quickstep or salsa, tango or cha-cha-cha.

In 1974 Cunard was the first company to provide speakers on board, on QE2. Then called the Festival of Life programme, it soon became a popular and regular feature on *Cunard Countess* and *Cunard Princess* as well.

Chris Frame, author and frequent on-board speaker recalls:

I was twenty-four at the time, the youngest ever enrichment lecturer to be aboard *QE2* in all her thirty-nine years, and had just spoken to a full house. Two days earlier we had been in Australia and had just flown in at the last minute as Cunard's guests to speak aboard. It was amazing. After the lecture there were lots of people coming over to talk to me. I knew I would get some tricky questions. It was, after all, a room full of experts, fans and people who loved *QE2*, so the interest was high. Right on cue a question from a gentleman up the back – "Chris, in the talk you said a special hypoxy liquid was used between the steel hull and the aluminium?" "Yes," I said. "Can you tell me the grade of metal used in the rivets that hold that join together?" Well of course, I was caught a bit off guard with the level of

Deck 3 on *QM2* offers board games and jigsaws to while away an hour or two at sea if the weather is inclement. (Sharon Poole)

Passengers on the aft deck of *QM2* are entertained by a live house band at lunchtime. (Andrew Sassoli-Walker)

detail requested. Just then, a little voice in the background said, "I know the answer to that question." There was a Scotsman who answered the question in immense detail. I was thrilled and asked him afterwards how he knew such exquisite detail of the ship's construction. Turns out, he was the man who drove those rivets into the hull of the ship! He came to all of my talks and fielded all of the questions that only people who built the ship would know the answer to!

Over the years Cunard ships have carried many major stars of stage and screen. In the days before affordable, convenient air travel, the ocean liner was the only way to cross and the 'only way to cross' was on Cunard, as their advertising boasted. Regular travellers included Walt Disney (who always reserved the same dining table on *Queen Elizabeth* because of its views of Manhattan), Cary Grant (who arranged his schedules around the timetable of the *Queen Mary* so he could always travel on her) and Bing Crosby (who spent many hours with the photographers, chatting in the refuge of their darkrooms, away from the attention of fans). Some famous passengers were happy to provide impromptu shows for fellow guests – Jerry Lewis and Dean Martin for example – and gradually Cunard formalised this arrangement. In the subsequent years, many famous actors, politicians, musicians, and captains of industry provided master classes, workshops and lectures and this continues today.

Royal Academy of Dramatic Arts (RADA) workshops, popular on *QM2*, were extended across the fleet in 2008. RADA graduates pass on theatrical tips, behind the scenes secrets and other coaching, with special workshops for younger travellers.

Among the vast range of entertainment on board the Cunard fleet today, the most innovative is probably the Planetarium on *QM2*. Installed in the centre of Illuminations, passengers relax on reclining seats while the ceiling lowers to provide a totally immersive experience. There are four shows daily, using cutting-edge technology to provide a virtual tour of space. Illuminations was also the first cinema at sea to show 3D films, in 2011.

Like most cruise ships, Cunard held art auctions on board for many years. These offered passengers the opportunity to purchase new and interesting pieces from both up-and-coming and established artists. About three years ago, the franchise to sell art on board the fleet was awarded to Clarendon Galleries, this time in the form of permanent galleries with changing displays of art in a variety of media.

The innovative and unique planetarium is built into illuminations on *QM2*. (Cunard)

The majority of the artwork on board Cunard ships are originals, with a few limited edition prints. On world cruises, as well as during the summer and autumn, artists often travel on the ships giving talks and demonstrations – Philip Gray even did an amazing painting underwater in one of the swimming pools using oil-based paints. Art Consultant Fenella Fay recalled some of her most interesting moments were with the German passengers. Since her grasp of the language is limited, on one occasion both sides ended up drawing on pieces of paper for nearly three hours! The art consultants are not just there to deal with sales, but also give talks on art history, often linking themes such as Impressionism with modern-day artists working in similar styles.

Artist Sheree Valentine-Daines paints a portrait of Captain Chris Wells, live before an audience on the maiden voyage of *Queen Elizabeth* in October 2010. (Sharon Poole)

Chapter 7

WINTER

As winter arrives, the ships head for the warmth of the Caribbean or north to the Christmas markets of Europe. Winter transatlantic crossings allow for some pre-Christmas shopping in New York City, a show or two on Broadway and then back in time for the holidays. Unfortunately, it can also bring some winter weather! In December 2013 the UK news reported that due to 30-foot waves off the Isle of Wight, the pilots on the departing cruise ships took their passports with them, in the event they couldn't get back onto the pilot launches!

Christmas on board may be a relaxing time for passengers but not for the crew, who, as with many professions, have to carry on much as normal. The ships are decorated by external contractors on a turnaround day early in December.

On board, the chefs prepare for the annual festive onslaught! The stores managers have to be on top of ordering extra supplies – turkeys, Christmas puddings and other seasonal delicacies. It is tradition for all the ships to display a gingerbread village. This is made in advance entirely from edible foodstuffs – marzipan, chocolate, icing and sweets – and assembled overnight, appearing as if by magic to passengers.

Christmas proper starts in the Royal Court Theatre with the Midnight Service on Christmas Eve, followed the next morning with the Captain's Service of Lessons and Carols, with readings from members of the ship's company. Santa Claus will appear at the top of the funnel and go to the Queens Room to hand out gifts to children. As in the Royal Navy, it is traditional for officers to serve lunch to the crew on Christmas Day. The Mess Halls are fully decorated, even down to Christmas crackers on the tables. Emphasising their British heritage, the Queen's Christmas Day speech is broadcast in the public rooms. Cunard afternoon tea is always special, but for Christmas Day the galley teams excel themselves with a Grand Afternoon High Tea, baking around 2,000 mince pies and twenty-four large Christmas cakes. In the evening there is a traditional Christmas Dinner with goose or turkey and all the trimmings followed by mince pies and Christmas pudding. The day will end with a Christmas Ball in the Queens Room as well as a show and other entertainments around the ship.

New Year's Eve is celebrated with a countdown in the Queens Room and parties across the fleet. One ship is usually in Funchal, Madeira, for the famous firework display.

Above left: Deck the halls, or in this case, the Grand Lobby of *QM2*, December 2013. (Sharon Poole)

Above: Christmas decorations in the form of Badger, Mole, Ratty and Mr Toad from *Wind in the Willows* on *QM2* in December 2013. (Sharon Poole)

Left and above right: The Christmas gingerbread village on *QM2*, December 2013. (Sharon Poole)

Above: After morning services, children (and many adults) go to the Queens Room to find Santa Claus as he passes out gifts on board *QM2* on Christmas Day 2013. This is repeated across the fleet. (Heather Dove)

Above right: The Britannia Restaurant on *QM2*, decorated for New Year's Eve in 2013. (Heather Dove)

Right: A New Year's Eve party in the Queens Room on *QM2*, 2013. (Heather Dove)

Queen Victoria leaving the harbour at Funchal, where P&O Cruises' *Azura* is still berthed, ready for the famous Madeiran New Year's Eve fireworks in 2012. (João Abreu)

Once the seasonal celebrations are over, the ships can turn their preparations to the world cruises. The first ship to offer a world circumnavigation was Cunard's *Laconia* in 1922 and from the start they were something very special. Commodore Sir Edgar Britten described the sense of anticipation and excitement perfectly.

On 1 January 1929, in command of the *Franconia*, I sailed away from the cold, grey climate of wintry New York to the sun-kissed lands of the warm South ... Sailing the Atlantic "Ferry" as I have done for the greater part of my life ... as the *Franconia* nosed her way down the broad waters of the Hudson I felt as happy as any of the eager, laughing holiday throng who crowded our decks. My chart-room was piled to the roof with charts, for we were to visit many strange places never touched before. There was no hurry ... just long lazy days of enchantment, drifting among strange islands in far-lying seas, skirting the coral reefs of Polynesia, cruising through narrow straits in spice-scented air, sailing ever to the East, chasing sunshine and happiness.

Franconia's cruise, from New York to New York, was an amazing 133 days. The cost – 405 guineas (£425) including all shore excursions or 305 guineas (£325) without!

Nowadays Cunard's world cruises and grand voyages generally start with a Southampton departure for the convenience of European passengers. Voyages vary each year with, usually, a full world cruise and a more targeted voyage such as Asia or South America. In 2015, Cunard's 175th anniversary year, all three ships will be offering a variety of world voyages, with *Queen Elizabeth* completing a full circumnavigation. *Queen Mary 2* will sail east through the Mediterranean to Asia and Australia, returning to the UK via South Africa, and *Queen Victoria* will travel west to New York and then south to the Caribbean, through the Panama Canal to Australasia and back via the west coast of the States, the Panama Canal,

New York and Southampton. Sectors are available for those who cannot spare three months away from home and work.

The itinerary planning generally takes place eighteen to twenty months ahead while the onboard work begins about six months in advance, when information has to be gathered as to what documentation and visas are required. These apply to crew as well as passengers so it is vital information is correct and up-to-date. Even if someone stays on board they will still be in that country's waters and so require the correct papers.

Anne Taylor accompanied her father Len around the world on *QM2* in 2011 for his eightieth birthday treat. She recalls:

What an experience! From the moment we set foot on the magnificent ship in New York, we both knew that this was to be the most wonderful privilege and adventure. On Thursday 13 January, against the backdrop of a floodlit New York sky-line, the *QM2* set sail, closely followed by the other two Queens. Crowds of well-wishers sent us off in style and it was a really moving moment, one which we will both never forget (and it was -10 degrees!). On board, life was very grand and treats for the passengers flowed. What never ceased to amaze me was the generosity of the staff on board. Despite working long hours they still had time to assist, care and go out of their way to ensure our time spent with them was the best it possibly could be.

Days passed, the wonderful cuisine got better and better and the waistline wider and wider! The temperature rose dramatically and two days after New York we were basking in the sunshine! The ambience on board ship was second to none, total pampering and relaxation throughout! My Dad's eightieth birthday could not have been better. Wall to wall sunshine mixed with champagne! Who could have asked for more!

Those travelling the full world cruise had their own area where they could get together and get to know one another, although the ironing room was the best place to meet!

QE2, probably the most famous and iconic ship of her age, is seen here about to depart on her last ever world cruise from Southampton in January 2007. (Andrew Sassoli-Walker)

Heavy snow provides an unusual view of the promenade deck of *QM2* at Brooklyn, New York, on her arrival back from the Caribbean Christmas and New Year Cruise in January 2014. (Heather Dove)

Above left: QM2 arrives for her maiden call at San Francisco on 4 February 2007. (Cunard)

Above: Queen Victoria, berthed beside the world-famous Sydney Harbour Bridge on a world cruise. (Chris Frame)

Left: Sydney Opera House as seen from the Promenade Deck of *Queen Victoria.* (Chris Frame)

The voyage was truly magnificent. Weekly cocktail parties added to the magical experience and we wondered if we would ever adjust to normal life again. The trip had its share of challenges for the Commodore (who was due to retire at the end of the world cruise): an earthquake on arrival at New Zealand, a tsunami when arriving in Japan and the political problems in Egypt. However, he took it all in his stride, and we sailed in safety throughout.

People have asked me over and over to tell them the best part of the trip. There wasn't any single best part, it was totally magnificent throughout! I am now saving hard to do the trip again when I am eighty – only thirty years to go!

With the ships far from home, communication networks become even more important. Business analyst at Carnival UK Niel Hilawi explains:

Offering good wireless coverage at sea is, increasingly, an almost exponential problem. The question starts with, what is the wireless service for? The immediate and obvious interpretation is access to the Internet. This implies connectivity to the great wide world while in the middle of the sea and without any cabled connections to land. To do this requires a bit of an Internet on board which is converted into a radio wave that goes from the ship, 33,000 miles up into the sky to be bounced back down another 33,000 miles by a satellite to some earth station, usually Goonhilly in Cornwall or others dotted around the globe, where it is then converted back into another form of communication which reconnects to the Internet. And for every single action on your computer there are a multitude of messages passing back and forth. Many of these satellites have been up in the sky longer than the Internet has existed and have not kept pace with the volume, speed and capacity that we are used to on land-based networks. There are newer ones but it's a never ending game of catch up. The volume of data that can be transferred is often referred to as 'bandwidth' and this implies the maximum amount of information that can be sent at any one moment in time. There is a great deal of competition for this space and time. As well as the guests and the ship's crew communicating with family, surfing the internet and checking their bank account, the ship's staff and IT systems are communicating at a business level with the office – email, business IT systems replicating data, business security and a host of other support activities all requiring twenty-four hours a day, seven days a week unfettered connectivity between ship and shore.

Special cake made for the start of the world cruise on *QM2* in 2011. (Anne Taylor)

On board, meanwhile, we are using wireless increasingly to great effect – passenger order-taking, access to on-board information systems and shipboard voice and messaging communications. Wireless technologies have provided considerable benefits in the speed of accessing/sending information and at the same time, cutting back considerably on costly cabling.

With the huge growth of computerisation both ashore and at sea, it is no surprise that the relatively new role of Electro-Technical Officer (ETO) was created to head up a team of support specialists for the electronic and electrical equipment on board today's vessels. In the past this role would have been undertaken by one of the engineering officers, who would act as the electrical specialist, while a Radio Officer might look after the limited amount of electronic equipment that was carried, such as the radar or echo sounder, in addition to his normal communications work. Nowadays the post of Radio Officer is defunct as communication equipment has become more user-friendly and no longer requires a familiarity with Morse code. The ETO's responsibilities cover all the electronic and electrical equipment, from those which control air conditioning through the vast amount of lighting and sound technology in the entertainment venues to that in the galleys and shops.

Until the 1970s, liners were taken out of service once a year for a refit and repairs. Nowadays, with longer maintenance schedules, this occurs every four years, with other work completed on a continuous cycle while the vessel is in service. At refit, the opportunity is often taken to make changes to the vessel. In October 2009 *QM2* sailed to the Blohm & Voss yard in Hamburg for three weeks dry docking before her fifth birthday season. Among various cosmetic updates, her hull was given a new anti-friction coating. She was also given increased wireless connectivity so passengers can use their own equipment throughout the ship. In May and June 2014 *Queen Elizabeth* underwent her first refit. Over twenty days, as well as general maintenance, nine new single staterooms were created, reflecting the changing demographics of passengers. Externally, new awnings were installed on the sun decks and the Lido restaurant was remodelled. On the technical side, a new filtration system for the exhaust gas from the ship's engines was installed to minimise environmental impact. Strict new emissions regulations are coming into force in various parts of the world, requiring this change.

Conditions have changed a great deal over the years regarding officer and crew accommodation. In the 1920s, deck-hands, for example, still shared a forecastle with up to thirty crew mates, sleeping in wooden double-tiered bunks with a small table and two benches between them all. By the 1950s, crew shared four-berth cabins with communal washing facilities and there was a crew library and lounge for their limited leisure hours. Nowadays things are very different, not only in terms of accommodation but also facilities. The crew mess serves meals not so different from those the passengers will be eating a few decks above. The officers' wardrooms offer a relaxing place to unwind and all Cunarders still have the famous Pig & Whistle, as the crew bar is known. There is also a crew gym and deck area with swimming pool.

Hotel operations are, from a passenger's point of view, some of the most important in ensuring they have a comfortable and memorable holiday. While the deck officers and engineers sail the ship, the hotel staff service the cabins, look after the entertainment and provide the food and drink. In charge of this operation is the Hotel General Manager. For them a typical day, if there can be such a thing, starts around 07:00 or earlier if in port, and ends between 22:00 and 23:00, with a well-earned break mid-afternoon. Between those times, there will be meetings, inspections, reports and appraisals to carry out. They head up a large team, most of whom will have learnt their trade at one of the White Star training schools set up all over the world. Cunard ships have some thirty-seven different nationalities among the crew. The Purser's Office is the busiest department, next to catering. They deal with all passenger queries, billing, etc. and are the first point of contact for all guest enquiries.

Safety is a priority on all ships and perhaps none more so than Cunard. From the beginning, the instructions to captains were to prioritise safety above all else. Indeed, when Dr Joseph Maguire, then senior doctor on board the *Queen Mary*, enquired why the ship never flew the Blue Riband pennant (awarded to ships holding the record for the fastest Atlantic crossing) he was told that the company never boasted of the speed of its ships, but rather the safety.

In the past a sea voyage was often prescribed for invalids and those of a delicate constitution. All passenger ships had to carry a doctor from the early nineteenth century, not least to deal with quarantine matters since a variety of contagious diseases were rife among all populations at that time. Nurses to assist them were not introduced until the 1930s. Nowadays ships' Medical Centres can cope with most emergencies, but do not have the staff for long-term treatment and care will only be given until the patient can be moved to an appropriate hospital ashore. Normally this would be at the next port, but occasionally the matter is more urgent and requires a helicopter evacuation. This decision is made between the Captain, senior doctor and Cunard's medical officer ashore.

On the third day of an eastbound transatlantic crossing in August 2009, *QM2* diverted from her course and ran north-west at full speed throughout the afternoon and into the night. As she reached a point some 200 miles off the coast of Newfoundland, a Canadian Hercules military transport aircraft began dropping flares around the ship before a large helicopter appeared over *QM2*. Two Canadian Coast Guardsmen were lowered and, working with *QM2*'s crew, placed a critically ill passenger into a stretcher. As quickly as it had appeared, the helicopter disappeared into the gloom. The next day, Commodore Bernard Warner announced that the passenger was resting comfortably in hospital. The officer in charge of this operation was Captain Robert Camby, then Deputy Captain of *QM2*. The evacuation of passengers from cruise ships by helicopter is becoming increasingly common as technology advances. Nonetheless, they are complex operations that require extensive planning and coordination. Captain Camby explains:

The facilities on board are second to none for a ship but they do not equate to the facilities at a land-based hospital. We don't have an operating theatre on board and some of the guests that we have disembarked by helicopter needed surgery. The first step is a determination by the ship's doctor that a person needs land-based care and must have it before the ship can reach port. Safety of life comes above anything so we will temporarily postpone the voyage to get the passenger off. The next step is for the doctor to call the bridge. Although technology keeps improving, a helicopter's range only extends some 200 miles out to sea, so the ship's navigator must determine if the ship can come within helicopter range within the time that the doctor believes is critical for the patient. Once the ship's master determines that a helicopter evacuation is necessary and feasible without placing others at an inordinate risk, the deputy captain becomes responsible for executing the operation. On a transatlantic crossing, this usually involves working with the British or Irish coastguards if the ship is in the eastern North Atlantic and the Canadian or US coastguards if the ship is closer to North America. I phone the coastguard station for the area that we are in and tell them it is a go. We will then communicate with them every thirty minutes to tell them our position, course and speed as well as updates on weather conditions such as the cloud cover and height, visibility, wind and whether the barometer is rising or falling. All the heads of department will then meet on the bridge, where we will refer to the ship's written procedures with regard to helicopter operations. These include the evacuation of certain cabins, the clearing of all the balconies of any debris, clearing of all open decks and manning of every single door to open decks. The reason that doors have to be secured and cabins and balconies evacuated is that there is always some risk involved when the ship is in close quarters with a helicopter. Accordingly, the preparations include setting up of all the fire teams up on Deck 13. Then we have some of our fast rescue boats manned so if anyone fell into the sea we would be able to rescue them. For all these reasons, passengers are not allowed to watch. One person, however, does stand on the open deck; the deputy captain is the flight deck officer and will co-ordinate the operation from the centre of the flight deck. He is the only one permitted to stand underneath the helicopter and communicates directly with the helicopter and the bridge. As mentioned earlier, there may also be a Hercules military transport plane. They act as a reconnaissance aircraft and do all the initial communication with us. If it is dark they drop flares, which will give the helicopter a runway approach to the ship. When the helicopter arrives, it does not land on the ship but hovers low over the deck. They will normally send down two people, a paramedic and a winchman, via a cable. They will be taken straight to where the patient will have been moved. At that stage, the helicopter moves off and stands by at the side of the ship. The paramedics transfer the patient from the stretcher in which they were brought up from the medical centre to their own equipment. Then the deputy captain will let the helicopter know they can make their approach again and we will bring the patient out onto the open deck. The paramedic will attach himself to the stretcher and he will go off with the patient. If the patient is travelling with a partner and they wish to go as well, they will go off with the winchman. Although this ends the ship's involvement in the evacuation, Cunard has established Care Teams to assist evacuated passengers and their families.

In addition to being responsible for medevacs of passengers, the Deputy Captain would also take a leading role in the unlikely event that there had to be an evacuation of the ship.

The best lifeboat is the ship itself so we would stay on board the ship as long as possible. We have food supplies, blankets and the ability to communicate. Even though the lifeboats have that as well, there is a possibility that people may get wet and hypothermia can then become a danger. In the event that a catastrophe required the evacuation of the ship, we have the ability with the GMDSS equipment to communicate with every

An RAF Sea King Search & Rescue helicopter from 22 Squadron evacuates a passenger requiring urgent medical treatment. (Sharon Poole)

living soul on the planet. Aircraft could arrive fairly fast and they would be able to drop extra life rafts and supplies before other ships arrived. Nowadays, the world is very small.

As is pointed out during every passenger lifeboat drill, fire is arguably the biggest threat to any ship. As such, the preventive measures in place are elaborate. Every area has at least two escape routes and there are a variety of detection systems in place. All cabins have sprinkler systems and, following a serious incident aboard *Star Princess* in 2006, all balcony furniture and curtains are now fire resistant and drenching systems are fitted to all balconies. Immediately any alarm is raised an assessment party, usually consisting of an officer, engineer and electro-technical officer, is despatched to the area to find out the type and severity of any fire. Meanwhile, a fire-fighting party under the control of the coxswain will be donning protective clothing and gathering appropriate equipment. In ninety-nine per cent of cases they will not be required to do anything further but no alarm, however minor it may at first appear, is ever regarded as such until known. If an alarm is raised in a passenger cabin, the first response is to phone that cabin, as sometimes it can be caused by steam from the shower. If there is no response, the twelve cabins either side are phoned and alerted to evacuate their cabins until it is deemed safe to return. Cunard ships have a system of smoke detectors linked to a hydrafog system that can blanket an area in a fire-dousing mist within seconds. The fire teams on board are all qualified and trained by the same fire training schools in the UK as normal land-based fire-fighters. All officers are trained fire-fighters and their tickets are refreshed every year when they get trained in the latest equipment. There are fire drills twice a month as well as familiarisation training for fire teams about every four days. The fire teams are drilled over and over again in entry procedures for a fire in any particular area to a point where they are as familiar with the ship as they are with their own home.

A Computer Safety System (CSS) enables the bridge team to constantly monitor all of the systems throughout the ship and gives them a visual alert to any potential situation. As on any modern vessel, all watertight doors, fire doors, emergency low-level lighting and ventilation can be operated from both the bridge and engine control room.

Nowadays, any incident on any ship has to be reported internationally to try and prevent a reoccurrence. A Safety Bulletin will be issued by the Marine Accident Investigation Branch. For example, when there was an incident where a cable snapped during a lifeboat exercise on *Thomson Majesty*, the exact cause, type of equipment being used, even down to the brand of grease used to lubricate it, was issued worldwide and checked against that being used by Cunard.

Carnival UK has established an Operational Support Centre, open 24/7, for when shore-based specialist advice is required for any reason. Nowadays with social media, companies need to be alerted much faster to any incidents. Captain Willard cited an example of a captain being alerted by telephone in his cabin to an incident. By the time he reached the bridge, the incident was all over Facebook. Shore-side managers had read the Facebook messages and were on the phone to him before he had even been briefed as to what had happened.

Every year the ships are inspected by the Flag state and Lloyds before the Passenger Safety Certificates can be renewed. These certificates, which allow ships to carry passengers, are only valid for twelve months. In order to achieve renewal, the vessels will be inspected by two surveyors over a period between seven and ten days. The inspection is very thorough, testing every safety item – fire screen doors, fire flaps, fog systems, sprinkler systems, fire pumps, bilge pumps, oily water separators, etc. They will also witness a full fire and boat drill plus abandon ship. Divers will review the hull condition with cameras so that the surveyor can see if there is any unseen damage or issues that may require attention.

Left: A life raft is tested while *Queen Elizabeth* is berthed at Tenerife on her maiden voyage in 2010. (Sharon Poole)

Right: Full abandon ship exercise on *QM2* while berthed at Zeebrugge in 2010. (Sharon Poole)

CONCLUSION

As Cunard reaches the milestone of its 175th anniversary, the popularity of this most iconic of brands has not waned, indeed it has increased – quite an achievement in this modern world and with a fleet of just three ships! Whether in Southampton, New York, Hamburg, Liverpool, or any other port around the world, spotting the iconic livery with black-topped funnels towering over the cranes and rooftops always provides a shiver of anticipation. Long may it continue.

Every day at noon the ship's bell is sounded in a small ceremony on *QM2*, July 2009. (Sharon Poole)

BIBLIOGRAPHY

Ships Monthly, November 1987, pp. 33–35

Bird, James, *The Major Seaports of the United Kingdom*, Hutchinson, 1969

Britten, Commodore Sir Edgar, *A Million Ocean Miles*, Hutchinson & Co., 1938

Edington, Sarah, *The Captain's Table*, National Maritime Museum Publishing, 2005

Fox, Stephen, *The Ocean Railway*, Harper Perennial 2003

Frame, Chris and Rachelle Cross, *Queen Victoria: A Photographic Journey*, The History Press, 2010

Harnack, Edwin (ed.), *All About Ships & Shipping*, Faber & Faber Ltd, 1934

Maguire, Dr Joseph, *The Sea My Surgery*, William Heinemann Ltd, 1957

Payne, Stephen, *RMS Queen Mary 2: Owners Workshop Manual*, Haynes Publishing, 2014

Prior, Rupert (comp.), *Ocean Liners: The Golden Years*, Tiger Books International, 1993

Queen Mary 2, The PPI Group, 2004

Queen Elizabeth, REM Productions, 2010

Wills, Elspeth, *Cunardia*, The Open Agency, 2005

All the Cunard ships have displays celebrating the rich history of the company. This is the Cunardia area on *Queen Victoria*, seen in 2009. (Sharon Poole)

ACKNOWLEDGEMENTS

The authors wish to extend their grateful thanks to all those who have kindly provided advice and assistance in writing this book and in particular, Captain Andrew Willard, Captain Robert Camby, Captain Ian McNaught MNM, Trevor Connelly, Dr Stephen M. Payne, Fenella Fay, Commodore Ronald Warwick rtd, Commodore Bernard Warner rtd, Chris Frame, João Abreu, Heather Dove, Caryll Young, Andrew Cooke, Fay Jordan, Howard Paulman, Vitor Francisco, Christian Reay, Anthony Marshall, Robert Neal Marshall, Tom Gulbrandsen, Anne Taylor and Richard Okill. Thanks are also due to Louis Archard at Amberley Publishing.